CW01651256

Portuguese Property Guide

Vedna Gavaloo
João Gil Figueira
Marisa Leitão dos Santos

First edition published in 2007

Although every effort has been made to ensure the accuracy of the information contained in this guide, as of the date of publication, nothing herein should be construed as giving legal advice. Obviously, the law is subject to change, and it changes very often in Portugal. In addition, the application of the law to specific circumstances can present complex issues that are beyond the scope of this guide. This publication is intended to provide general legal information pertaining to investing in property and living in Portugal. CAMEIRA LAW, London would be delighted to provide more detailed information upon request and may be contacted at the addresses provided on the back cover.

Paperback ISBN 978104312956
Published in the UK by MX Publishing
335, Princess Park Manor, Royal Drive, London, N11 3GX.

CONTENTS

FOREWORD

This new edition of the Portuguese Property Guide bears the distinction of being a very resourceful guidance to those who are interested in the real estate industry in Portugal.

Portugal has long been a prime destination for foreign second-home buyers. At a time when property markets in other countries are stagnating, Portugal seems to be very much on the up. On a practical level, Portugal is an exceptionally pleasant place to live and certainly lures back scores of holidaymakers, year after year.

The aim of this guide is to assist you to make informed decisions and overcome the obstacles that so often infuriate people finding their way in the property maze. The guide is dedicated to assist you in realising your goals, budget and buying timetable and to secure a property. With a wealth of authoritative editorial and guidance, the Portuguese Property Guide is a standalone primer to anyone interested in acquiring real estate in Portugal.

Diogo Tavares de Carvalho
Managing Partner – Lisbon Office
Tavares de Carvalho & Associados – Sociedade de Advogados R.L.

ACKNOWLEDGEMENTS

The authors wish to express their deepest gratitude to Maria Antónia Cameira and Diogo Tavares de Carvalho for their considered professional advice and invaluable input at all stages in the production of this guide. Without their assistance it would not have been possible.

PART I: WORKING AND LIVING IN PORTUGAL

1. INTRODUCTION

Portugal has a rich seafaring past and it is one of Europe's unspoilt gems with its land of traditional villages, vibrant cities and a countryside strewn with historical treasures. It is one of the quieter holiday home investment destinations and hence, remains even today, partly undiscovered.

A member-country of the European Union since 1986, Portugal enjoys a steady economic growth and it is one of the most cost-effective countries in which to live in Europe. With food and wine inexpensive coupled with first-class healthcare services, a high quality of life is readily achievable. This dynamic and emerging country is utterly equipped with a network of well-developed infrastructure and a globally competitive work force. For centuries, Portugal has indisputably kept the greatest treasure of a renowned reputation for hospitality that makes the country a haven of congeniality and safety.

During the last decade, vast swathes of the Portuguese coastline have been developed in a construction boom. Many other places in Portugal have benefited from the continued strength of the property market, and as the market becomes more structured and transparent to buyers, interest is starting to shift away from the holiday "hot spots" into the relatively untouched beauty of the countryside. The market has a great deal to offer for those looking to relocate to the country and there is the opportunity to acquire a fairly priced property that should perform well in the future. Portugal real estate is a stable investment market and property sales are, bucking the trends with Britons in particular.

The right of ownership of property in Portugal is well protected and the planning permission is subject to rigorous controls, in an attempt to avoid the overdevelopment that has blighted other parts of Europe.

On the western edge of mainland Europe, Portugal has eye-catching landscapes and scenery. Nearly 1000 kilometres of coastline carves up the country's interior from the Atlantic Ocean, affording visitors some of European's most spectacular and pristine beaches.

The Silver Coast remains raw and untouched and has long been heralded as the real Portugal with minuscule villages, stunning inland towns and close proximity to beaches. This region of Portugal offers investors cultural and historical buildings, astounding monasteries, majestic cathedrals and legionary fortresses. The appeal is evident to the savvy investor. Following in the footsteps of the Algarve, developers along the Silver Coast have also begun constructing world class golf courses to cash in on Portugal's lucrative sports to tourism market.

Retrospective and innovative, Lisbon is a twilight zone between past and future with its dodgem-like trams screech through cobbled streets. Historically and culturally Lisbon is incredibly rich – it dates back to pre-Roman times and embodies Portugal's unique culture and charm which has been moulded by generations of invaders and rulers from diverse cultures and backgrounds. Naturally the city is one of the most affluent parts of Portugal and it has high levels of inward migration both nationally and internationally. Portuguese folk music or Fado can be echoed throughout Lisbon, but for those who don't relate to the doleful lyrics and music there are concerts of music across the city embracing all genres, there are an abundance of bars, of restaurants serving an array of scrumptious foods.

Blessed with steady sunshine, the Algarve is laced with luscious landscapes, stupendous beaches and astonishing golfing facilities. The natural attractions of Portugal enable the country to sustain a steady influx of holidaymakers, expats, retirees, professional workers and investors. After the magnetism of the landscape, you can indulge in the exquisite aromas and flavours of the traditional Algarve cuisine. Only one stride from the tranquil peace of inland region is the thrill of an incredible nightlife.

This informative guide is a "must have" as it will take readers through the essentials of living in Portugal and it will give them the inside scoop on how to avoid the traps and pitfalls of the Portuguese property market.

2. LEGAL REGIME OF ENTRY AND RESIDENCE IN PORTUGAL

2.1 Right of Entry

2.2.1 EU Nationals

Following the EU Directives transposition into the Portuguese Legal framework, all EU nationals wishing to settle in Portugal (whether for the purposes of employment, self-employment, provision of services, studies or retirement), are no longer required to obtain a visa in order to reside in Portugal. In effect, EU Nationals may travel, circulate and work freely in any Member State, enjoying the same rights as citizens of the host country. Family members are also entitled to free circulation, irrespective of their nationality.

Consequently EU Nationals have the right to carry out a professional activity in Portugal, under either an employed or self-employed regime, without the need to apply for a work permit, and also enjoy the same rights as Portuguese workers as regards salary, working conditions, access to lodging, vocational training , social assistance and trade union rights.

Thus, an EU National is allowed to enter in Portugal, without complying with any other formality, other than possessing a valid identificatory (passport or identity card). Nevertheless, where the intended stay in Portugal is greater than 3 months, it is advisable to apply for a Residence Card, a simple administrative procedure certifying status as an EU National.

Family members of an EU National, who are not EU Nationals, will not require entry visas, however they will have to comply with specific entry formalities. A family member is any of the following persons: spouse, common law spouse (registered), direct descendants or stepchildren younger than 21 years old. They should notify the competent authorities in their home jurisdiction of their presence in the Portuguese territory.

Swiss nationals have the same rights as EU nationals regarding entry and residence in Portugal.

2.2.2 Non-EU Nationals

Non-EU nationals must apply personally, at a Portuguese Consulate in their country of origin or residence, for entry visas. The Portuguese Consulate General in the UK is located at 3 Portland Place, London W1B 1HR, Tel 020 7291 3770.

In order to obtain an entry visa it is necessary to present the following documents:

(i) 2 passport photographs;
(ii) Evidence of economic self-sufficiency (i.e. adequate personal funds to support oneself without recourse to public funds);
(iii) Travel insurance; and
(iv) The Applicant's Passport must be valid 3 months beyond the intended stay.

The entry visa is valid for a maximum period of 4 months, depending on the nationality of the beneficiary. The visa may be extended.

2.2 Right to Reside in Portugal

2.2.1 EU Nationals

EU Nationals who intend to live in Portugal for a period exceeding 3 months, must formalise their right of residence by registering within 30 days of the end of their first three months in the country, at the Municipal Council in which they live, or at the respective Delegation of the Foreigners and Borders Service (*Serviço de Estrangeiros e Fronteiras - SEF*), or at the *Loja do Cidadão (Citizen Shop).* When they register, they are issued with a Registration Certificate, which is valid for 5 years. In order to obtain the Registration Certificate it is necessary to present the following documents:

(i) Valid identity card or passport;

(ii) A declaration under oath, that Applicants fulfil the following pre-requisites :

a) To carry out a professional activity in Portugal, under either an employed or self-employed regime. Self-employed individuals will need to present documents proving an established status in Portugal (for example, commercial registration and tax payer's number); and
b) They have sufficient income to support themselves and their dependants without recourse to the Portuguese social assistance system.
c) Job-seekers, students and pensioners will have to present proof of adequate resources to be self-sufficient without the need to rely on the Portuguese social assistance system during their period of residence and have comprehensive sickness insurance cover in Portugal.

EU family members must also apply for a Registration Certificate. They must present proof of identification, the Registration Certificate of the main European Applicant and proof of their family relationship.

Non-EU family members must formalise their right of residence by applying for a Residence Card at the Central Services or Regional Delegation of the Foreigners and Borders Service (*Serviço de Estrangeiros e Fronteiras – SEF*), which is nearest to their place of residence. The following documentation will be required:

(i) 2 passport photographs;
(ii) Valid passport;
(iii) Register Certificate, Residence Card or Identification Card of the main European Applicant they are accompanying;
(iv) Proof of their family relationship and guardianship, if applicable.

The Registration Certificate and the Residence Card of the EU citizens' family members will be given the same validity as that of the main European Applicant.

- **Permanent Residence Certificate/Card**

EU nationals and their family members, who have been living in Portugal for 5 consecutive years, may request a Permanent Residence Certificate/Card, upon presentation of a valid Residence Certificate/Card to the *SEF*. They will henceforth be entitled to reside in Portugal without the need to comply with any further formality. The request must be presented to *SEF* before the Residence Card expires.

The right of permanent residence can be lost through absence from Portuguese territory for a period exceeding 2 consecutive years.

2.2.2 Non-EU Nationals

Non- EU Nationals must apply personally, at a Portuguese Consulate of the area where they live, for a residence visa. The following documentation will be required:

(i) A return ticket assuring the applicant's return to the country of origin;
(ii) Proof of accommodation in Portugal;
(iii) A contract or promissory contract of employment or services;
(iv) A Portuguese Social Security declaration attesting the status of the Applicant;
(v) A Criminal Record check issued by the competent authorities, either emanating from the country of origin or the country of residence (if living there for over 1 year).

3. PROOF OF IDENTITY

It is a legal requirement for individuals in Portugal to carry with them at all times some form of identification. A Portuguese national would be expected to show his/her identification card, but such cards are no longer issued to foreign nationals and it would therefore be acceptable for a British national to produce his residence card or passport. A driver's licence or credit card would not be considered sufficient proof of identity.

An individual who is unable to show an acceptable form of identification to the authorities on demand will be given 6 hours within which to do so. The police can detain anyone who is unable to produce satisfactory identification until such a time as his/her identity has been established.

4. IMPORTATION OF PERSONAL BELONGINGS

If the intention is to settle in Portugal, personal belongings (i.e. household effects, tools, bicycles, camping equipment, intended solely for personal use and consumption) may be imported duty-free, provided such belongings have been in use in the country of origin for at least 6 months prior to departure. Imported goods such as caravans, yatchts or other motor vehicles may have been in use in the country of origin for at least 12 months prior to departure. It is trite law that the imported goods cannot be subjected to any assignment, leasing or loan for at least 12 months following the date of importation. Electrical goods which are identifiable by serial number must be declared to the custom officials.

The company handling relocation will deal with the formalities itself and it is therefore essential to appoint an experienced international mover.

Further information can be obtained from the nearest Portuguese Consulate or from the Portuguese Customs and Excise Authority, or a reputable agent. Information is also available in Portuguese on the *Direçcão-Geral's* website at www.dgaiec.min-financas.pt.

5. MOVEMENT OF PETS

5.1 Movement of Pets from an EU Member State

Pets brought to Portugal from another Member State must be accompanied by a passport which must include a health certificate (*Atestado Sanitário*) issued by the competent authority in the country of origin. The certificate should state that the pet is in good health and does not come from a region where contagious diseases, such as rabies, prevail. It should be translated into Portuguese and presented to the customs authorities on arrival in Portugal.

Dogs and cats must also have an identifying tattoo or an electronic identification system.

Pet passports are issued in Britain by the Department of Environment, Food and Rural Affairs, Noble House, 17 Smith Square, London SW1 P 3JR.

If the veterinary authority in the country of origin requires an official notification in order to issue a health certificate, a request for such notification may be made to the *Direcção-Geral de Veterinária, Largo da Academia Nacional das Belas Artes 2, 1200-005 Lisboa (Tel 21 323 95 00*, e-mail: veterinaria@mail.telepac.pt).

An EU National may bring up to five pets into Portugal. If travelling with more than five animals, the owner must contact the *Direcção-Geral de Veterinária* for further advice.

Pet owners must carry a valid EU Pet Passport and the original vaccination certificates, for each pet when travelling with their animals to Portugal.
Portugal does not set any additional veterinary requirements for pet dogs and cats entering the country for non-commercial reasons. Animals do not have to be treated for ticks or tapeworm.

If the rabies vaccination was the animal's first vaccine then 21 days must pass before it may enter the country. There is no time delay with booster injections, providing there is proof that the booster was administered before the last vaccine had expired.

Dogs of dangerous types can be brought into Portugal provided that they are accompanied by their owners. The dogs must undergo sterilisation if the duration of their stay in Portugal exceeds 4 months.

Animals under three months old can only be brought into Portugal from an EU Member State if the owner can prove that young animals are not yet weaned and are accompanying the mother. If the animals are coming from outside the EU they must be over three months old.

5.2 Movement of Pets from outside an EU Member State

An animal entering Portugal from a non-EU country that has the same rabies controls needs:

- identification by microchip or tattoo; and
- valid anti-rabies vaccination;
- For a list of complying countries see website: www.ec.europa.eu

Animals from countries not included on the list need to have complete anti-rabies treatment in addition to the above. The neutralising antibody titration test is a system that combines vaccination against rabies and serological surveillance. The neutralising antibody titration (at least equal to 0,5 IU/ml) must be performed in an approved laboratory on a sample issued by a vet at least 30 days after the anti-rabies vaccination was given and three months before travel.

The Portuguese Embassy in the home country should be consulted or the *Direcção-Geral de Veterinária* prior to carrying out the importation. A vet will be able to manage the process.

6. COST OF LIVING

Characterising the cost of living of any country is naturally conditioned by two factors: location and lifestyle. Urban living clearly has nothing in common with living in a small town or countryside, where income and expenses associated with accessing facilities, are often entirely different. In Portugal, the prices tend to be higher in the coastal areas, especially large cities like Lisbon and Oporto, as well as the tourist resorts that are found in the Algarve.

Although the cost of living in Portugal is beginning to rise as the country falls into line with the rest of the EU, it remains one of the most economical countries in which to reside in Europe, where a high quality of life is easily achievable with relatively humble means.

The cost of living is considerably cheaper than in the UK, as follows:

Rents	€500 - €1,000 per month
Water rates	From €10 per month
Electricity	From €30 per month
Car tax	€7 – €350 per year
Petrol / Diesel	€1,20 per litre/ €1 per litre
Eating out	Under €20
Wine in restaurants	From €3 per bottle
Beer	From €1 per bottle
Gas	€22 per bottle

7. LIGHTING AND HEATING

Electric voltage in Portugal is 220volts AC, 50Hz. Wall sockets are of the standard European variety which consists of two round pins. Electricity is rarely used for cooking and while natural gas is becoming increasingly available, the use of butane gas dispensed in cylinders still prevails, and is quite economical.

Despite the brilliant outdoor sunshine, the interior of houses and flats often proves to be rather cold and damp during the winter and good heating is therefore essential. Some modern houses have central heating systems.

8. PROPERTY INSURANCE

Property insurance contracts may be entered into whether in Portugal or through a broker in the UK. Overseas property insurance is readily available in the UK and has the distinct advantage of disbursing payments on any claim, in sterling and in the UK.

9. DRIVING IN PORTUGAL

Drivers in Portugal must carry their identification, driving licence and vehicle documents at all times when on the road. All vehicles must have 2 warning triangles and all passengers in both front and rear are required to wear seatbelts.

Traffic police - the GNR or PSP - frequently carry out road checks and are able to issue and collect substantial 'on the spot fines' for failure to comply with these rules and other types of traffic offences.

Motorway users in Portugal are required to pay tolls to cover the cost of maintenance. Hefty fines are imposed on those who cannot pay on demand at toll collection gates.

The private companies that maintain the motorway system operate an automatic payment scheme (*Via Verde*) to make the passage through toll gates speedier. Subscribers to this scheme are issued with vehicle identification units and are entitled to use the green lane marked "V" at toll gates. Penalties are imposed for the unauthorised use of the "green lane".

10. DRIVERS' LICENCES

When taking up residence in Portugal it is possible to retain a UK driver's licence for a period of 6 months, following arrival.

However, there are a number of very good reasons for exchanging the licence for a Portuguese-issued one. These are:

- As in Britain, it is a legal requirement in Portugal for the address on the licence to reflect the correct address of its holder.
- If lost, stolen or damaged, the licence can only be renewed or replaced by the original issuing authority. Some licensing authorities, such as the DVLA, will not renew or replace a licence in connection with an overseas address.
- When the licence eventually expires, the Portuguese authority will not renew until such time as the holder takes and passes a driving test in Portugal.

A national driver's licence (old-style green model) must be exchanged for a Portuguese-issued licence.

In order to carry out the exchange, an application should be made to the nearest office of the *Direcção-Geral de Viação* (Portuguese Driver and Vehicle Licensing Agency). In such cases, it is a requirement to surrender the original.

11. IMPORTATION OF MOTOR VEHICLES

New and second-hand cars are readily available on a local basis, and therefore it is reasonable to consider buying a Portuguese-registered car in Portugal. Notwithstanding, vehicles can be imported duty-free from another Member State provided the owner was resident in that country prior to settlement in Portugal and tax on the vehicle has already been fully paid. Importation is often, however, a complicated and somewhat lengthy process.

11.1 Temporary Admission of Motor Vehicles

An EU-registered motor vehicle (including light goods vehicles, trailers, caravans, motor-homes and motorcycles) may be kept in Portugal for a continuous period of up to 180 days, provided the following community requirements are complied with:

- The vehicle is registered in the name of a person who is not resident in Portugal;
- The vehicle is brought into Portugal by its registered owner or keeper;
- The vehicle is for private use only;
- The vehicle is only driven by its registered owners or keepers provided they are neither established, resident nor employed in Portugal, and

- The vehicle's owner or keeper is in possession of the vehicle registration documents for presentation when necessary to the competent authority.

11.2 Permanent Importation of Motor Vehicles

For those who intend to set-up residence in Portugal, it is possible to import a motor vehicle tax-free, provided:

- The vehicle is for private use only;
- The registered owner of the vehicle is transferring his residence from another Member State where he has been resident for at least 185 days;
- The vehicle was purchased and fully tax-paid in its registered owner's former country of residence; and
- The vehicle has been used by its registered owner in his former country of residence for at least six months.

11.3 Importation Procedure

In order to import a vehicle, an application must be submitted within a maximum of 12 months following arrival, to the local customs office in the area of residence. These are as follows:

For those resident in the districts of Leiria, Lisbon, Portalegre and Santarém:

Alfândega de Lisboa
Jardim do Tabaco
Avenida Infante D Henriques
1100-280 Lisboa
Tel.: 21 881 3700 Fax: 21 881 3990

Braga, Bragança, Guarda, Porto, Viana do Castelo and Vila Real:

Alfândega do Freixieiro
Estrada Nacional 107
Perafita

4405-496 Matosinhos
Tel.: 22 999 9680/9690 Fax: 22 996 0725

Aveiro, Coimbra, Castelo Branco, Guarda and Viseu:

Alfândega de Aveiro
Apartado 931, Edifício TERTIFE, Lugar Moinhos
3801-301 Aveiro
Tel.: 23 4381153 Fax: 23 4381062-

Beja, Évora and Setúbal:

Alfândega de Setúbal
Avenida Jaime Rebelo
2904-536 Setúbal
Tel.: 26 552 1300 Fax: 26 523 4156

Algarve:

Alfândega de Faro
Avenida da República, 4
8000-079 Faro
Tel.: 28 980 1529 Fax: 28 989 8559

Madeira:

Alfândega do Funchal
Avenida do Mar e das Comunidades Madeirenses, 24
9000-054 Funchal
Tel.: 29 122 30576 Fax: 29 123 0156

Azores:

Alfândega de Ponta Delgada
Praça Vasco da Gama
9500-350 Ponta Delgada
Tel.: 29 628 7800 Fax: 29 628 4469

The application should be submitted together with:

- The vehicle's logbook;
- A certificate of compliance or Form 1402 issued by the *Direcção-Geral de Viação* (Portuguese DVLA) confirming that the vehicle has undergone inspection;
- Driver's licence;
- Evidence that application has been made for a residence card or else confirmation from the local Parish Council (*Junta de Freguesia*) of residency status within its jurisdiction;
- Taxpayer's identification card, together with 3-years' original tax returns or a declaration from the local tax office of the area of residence attesting to the amount of income earned in Portugal over the previous three years;
- A certificate attesting the establishment and cancellation of dates of residence issued by the competent authority in the former country of residence. (If, as in Britain, there is no such authority, the Consulate will issue a certificate on production of evidence that an application has been made for a residence card).

The authorities may request further documentation, as necessary, so it is advisable to contact them prior to submitting the application form, requesting a list of the necessary supporting documents and the applicable fees.

Following formal submission of the application, the customs authorities may issue a limited-validity authorisation (*guia de circulação*) which will enable use of the vehicle while the application is still under consideration.

A motor vehicle that has been imported in accordance with the abovementioned procedure cannot be sold, loaned, pledged or hired for a period of 12 months following importation. In addition, it may only be driven by its registered owners or keepers and their immediate family. The tax-free importation of motor vehicles is limited to one per person, every 10 years.

Companies such as FAOTIR will handle the vehicle importation process for a fee (Travessa Castilho 17 – 2º – Esq, 8000-457 Faro, Tel 00351 289 803 226, Fax 00351 289 821 718).

11.4 Motor Vehicle Documentation

All vehicles in Portugal are required to have:

- *Título de Registo de Propriedade* (Ownership Registration Document), issued by the *Conservatória do Registo Automóvel* (Vehicle Registration Office); and the
- *Livrete* (Vehicle Registration Document), issued by the *Direcção-Geral de Viação* (Portuguese Driver and Vehicle Licensing Agency - DGV); or
- *Certificado de Matrícula* (Vehicle Registration Certificate), issued by the DGV;
- Road Tax Payment. This is paid annually during the month in which the vehicle licence was issued and may also be obtained through the internet. The cost varies depending on the age and cubic capacity of the vehicle; and
- Insurance. All vehicles must have at least third party insurance cover. The insurance company will provide an insurance stamp for display in the lower right-hand corner of the vehicle's windscreen, at the time the policy is issued.

These documents, as well as the driver's ID and driver's licence, should be carried at all times for presentation to the authorities on request.

11.5 MOT Testing and Certificates

As in Britain, MOT testing is compulsory in Portugal for all vehicles. The test (*Inspecção Periódica Obrigatória* - IPO) must be carried out at an approved garage. The garage is required to request the vehicle's ownership document (*Título de Registo de Propriedade*), its logbook (*Livrete*) or the new Vehicle Registration Certificate, and the owner's taxpayer's identity card prior to carrying out the test.

A stamp confirming that the vehicle has undergone (and passed) the test will subsequently be issued. This should be displayed below the insurance stamp, in the lower right-hand corner of the vehicle's windscreen.

12. BANKING AND CURRENCY REGULATIONS

On January 1st 2002, euro notes and coins replaced the Portuguese Escudo. The Bank of Portugal will continue to exchange escudo notes and coins for a period of 30 years.

The Euro is divided into 100 cents. There are seven bank notes (€5, €10, €20, €50, €100, €200 and €500) and eight coins (1, 2, 5, 10, 20 and 50 cents and €1 and €2).

Both residents and non-residents may open a bank account in euros or any other foreign currency. Banks are open to the public from 08:30 until 15:00, Monday to Friday. The use of the *Multibanco* cash withdrawal machines is extensive and on-line banking is becoming increasingly popular.

There are several types of bank accounts similar to the UK. Branches of the Portuguese banks in London can be contacted for further information. However, where the account holder falls into the "resident" category, Portuguese income tax will become payable on any interest earned from any bank account held in Portugal.

There is no restriction on the amount of currency entering or leaving Portugal, but large sums of money should be transferred through proper banking channels.

13. HEALTH SERVICE

13.1. Portuguese National Health Service

The Portuguese Constitution is the supreme law of Portugal and protection in health is a fundamental right, which the Constitution guarantees to every citizen including foreign nationals. Health Centres and Hospitals are bound to provide assistance to immigrants in need of immediate healthcare irrespective of their nationality, economic or legal status in Portugal.

Everyone in Portugal is entitled to free national health services through the National Health Service (*Serviço Nacional de Saúde – SNS*), which encompasses public Hospitals and Health Centres (*Centros de Saúde*).

Healthcare in Portugal has improved tremendously in recent years, particularly in urban areas. Virtually everyone in Portugal has, or is, entitled to national health coverage through the *Serviço Nacional de Saúde* (SNS).

Each SNS area has a *Centro de Saúde*, similar to local day-time surgeries or clinics in UK terms, and each SNS beneficiary is for the time being obliged to use the clinic that comes within his/her area of residence.

There are 364 state-owned clinics and 488 first-aid points in mainland Portugal, 17 and 16 respectively in the Azores and 12 and 8 in Madeira.

In the event of requiring specialised treatment or operations, patients are referred to the appropriate specialist or hospital by the "family doctor" at the clinic, or his substitute. Referral works well but, as in the UK, there is a fairly long waiting list for operations. The maximum advisable delay time is said to be between 15 days and 2 months.

Most of the GPs and specialists are of Portuguese nationality and their standard is exceptionally high. All doctors practising conventional medicine must be registered with the *Ordem dos Médicos*, a body similar to the BMA.

Dental care is theoretically available under the national health schemes but the long waiting list means that private dental work is in great demand. Private dental work is expensive.

13.1.1 Obtaining a National Insurance Identity Card

To benefit from State medical treatment, foreign residents are required to obtain a Portuguese National Insurance Identity Card (*Cartão de Utente*) from their local Health Centre or *Loja do Cidadão*, prior to their enrollment with a General Practitioner ("GP"). The National Insurance Identity Card must be presented when booking medical appointments at clinics or purchasing prescription medicines in drugstores and pharmacies. Documentation required to be submitted are as follows:

- Work Permit; or
- Residence Card/Certificate

Until such time as a Residence Card/Certificate is issued, foreign residents will be entitled to medical treatment at any State health facilities, in case of emergency on production of their passport. Routine consultations and prescriptions for existing illnesses only become available once a residence card has been issued and an NHS card applied for.
Residents who are not in possession of a Work Permit or a Residence Card/Certificate can also apply for a National Insurance Identity Card by presenting a document attesting their status of residency in Portugal. The duration of the residence shall be at least 90 days and the said document can be obtained from the Parish Council.

Beneficiaries of the NHS are compelled to use the Health Centre within their catchment areas. In case of emergency or in the event of specialised treatment or operations, patients will be referred to the appropriate specialist or hospital by the respective GP.

13.2 British Citizens Working or Living in Portugal

Under the Protocol on Medical Treatment that was signed between Portugal and the UK on November 15th 1978, British citizens who are ordinarily resident in Portugal are entitled to state medical treatment on the same terms as any Portuguese national who is covered by the National Health Service. Non-resident British visitors to Portugal are entitled to emergency medical treatment at state facilities on production of their British passport.

In order to find out more about receiving a state pension while living abroad, Pension Services may be contacted at the International Pension Centre at Tyneview Park, Newcastle-upon-Tyne NE98 1BA, tel 0191 218 7777, fax 0191 218 7293, or alternatively their website consulted at www.thepensionservice.gov.uk.

a) Working in Portugal

British citizens working in Portugal and paying compulsory UK National Insurance contributions may be entitled, along with their dependants, to private healthcare paid by the UK.

If working abroad for less than a year, British citizens will need to contact HM Revenue and Customs in the UK in order to obtain an E101 form, as evidence to show that they are paying compulsory tax and national insurance in the UK. In case of prolonged stay, lasting longer than a year, British citizens may remain UK insured for a further 12 months, provided that a request is made before the form E101 expires.

If working abroad for 2 years or more (in a maximum of 5 years), the employer should contact the HM Revenue and Customs for the obtention of the aforementioned E101 form and, the E106 form, which would give assurance to British citizens and their respective family with the same level of medical care as Portuguese residents.

b) Living in Portugal

Those who are retired and are in receipt of a UK State retirement pension or long-term incapacity benefit may also be entitled to State healthcare paid by the UK if applying for an E121 form at the Overseas Healthcare Team.

British citizens receiving a UK pension may apply for a Portuguese National Insurance Identity Card and enrol with a state GP on arrival, simply on the production of their passport, pension receipts and the E121 form.

If British citizens live but do not work in Portugal and do not receive any UK benefits, they may be eligible for up to two-and-a-half years of State healthcare paid by the UK. They will have to apply for an E106 form with the Overseas Healthcare Team and prove that they have been working in the UK and paid national insurance contributions for up to 3 years before prior to their arrival in Portugal.

13.3 European Health Insurance Card (EHIC)

Irrespective of the travel motives, it is always advisable to obtain a European Health Insurance Card, before coming to Portugal.

The European Health Insurance Card is identical for all Europeans and can be obtained, free of charge. EHIC guarantees to all Europeans access to State health services, if any health problems arise in any Member State.

Additionally, any contributions by the patients for the cost of care will be reimbursed even after the patients return to their country of origin. The reimbursement can be obtained by either contacting the relevant branch of *Administração Regional de Saúde* or the Overseas Healthcare Team.

Treatment for maternal and child health, vaccination and chronic diseases, are free of charge in Portugal.

In the event of accident or serious disease in Portugal, the EHIC does not guarantee payment for travel fares to the home country. Therefore, it is highly recommended to purchase a travel insurance policy before travelling to Portugal.

For further information:

HM Revenue and Customs Charity, Assets and Residence
Address: Room BP1301 Benton Park View Newcastle upon Tyne NE98 1ZZ
Website: www.hmrc.gov.uk

UK National Health Service
Website: www.nhs.uk
Portal da Saúde
Website: www.portaldasaude.pt

Direcço-Geral da Saúde
Address: Alameda D.Afonso Henriques,45-1049-005 Lisboa
Tel: (+351) 21 843 05 00
Fax: (+351) 21 843 05 30
Website: www.dgs.pt **Email:** geral@dgs.pt

13.4 Prescribed Medicines

Prescribed medicines are sold at government controlled prices and national healthcare beneficiaries pay only a percentage of the authorised retail price, the remainder being paid by the State in a 95%, 69%, 37% or 15%, depending on their pharmaceutical classification and whether the prescribed medicines are considered vital for life. They are delivered pre-packed to the pharmacies ready for retail sale over the counter.

The packaging bears the manufacturer's name and address, the Portuguese registration number and the product's date of expiry and contains very detailed literature on the product, including side effects.

On the outside of the package there is a reference number which the pharmacist cuts out before handing over the medicine to the person presenting the prescription written by a state registered doctor. The number is then glued to the prescription which is retained by the pharmacy as proof of sale to the patient for whom it has been prescribed. The number is subsequently glued to the prescription which is retained by the pharmacy as proof of sale to the patient for whom it has been prescribed. In Portugal, non-prescription medicines are also available in supermarkets.

Patients suffering from chronic diseases are entitled to free medicine on prescription.

13.5 Alternative Medicines

Alternative Medicine is not recognised by the Portuguese *Ordem dos Médicos* (equivalent to the British Medical Association) and, is not available under NHS schemes. However, there is currently a strong move underway, encouraging the recognition of forms of manipulation such as acupuncture, chiropractic and osteopathy.

13.6 Private Healthcare

Private health insurance schemes are available through Portuguese and foreign Companies. Private health insurance schemes are available through Portuguese companies such as *Império* and Victoria and foreign companies such as BUPA. Many foreign residents take out private medical insurance as a safeguard.

There are several good but extremely expensive private clinics in Portugal. There is a British hospital in Lisbon which has both in- and out-patient facilities but it is not equipped to deal with major emergencies. Some of the nursing staff are British and all speak English. It is a private corporation.

PRIVATE HOSPITALS
(With in and out-patient facilities and which carry out medical examinations)

The British Hospital
Rua Tomás da Fonseca, Torre B
1600-209 Lisboa
Tel.(+351) 21 721 34 00
Fax (+351)21 721 34 39
Website: bh.gpsaude.pt
E-mail: info@mail.british-hospital.pt

Hospital da Cruz Vermelha
Rua Duarte Galvão, 54
1549-008 Lisboa
Tel: (+351) 21 044 61 84
Fax: (+351) 21 771 40 17
Website: www.cruzvermelha.pt
E-mail:geral@hcvp.com.pt

Hospital da CUF
Travessa do Castro, 3
1350-070 Lisboa
Website: www.josedemellosaude.pt

Hospital da Luz
Address: Avenida Lusíada, 100, 1500-650 Lisboa
Tel: (+351) 21 002 52 00
Fax: (+351) 21 002 52 20
Website: www.hospitaldaluz.pt
E-mail: geral@hospitaldaluz.pt

Hospital dos Lusiadas
Address: Alto dos Moinhos, 1500 Lisboa
Tel: (+351) 21 770 40 40
Fax: (+351) 21 770 40 81
Website: www.hppsaude.pt
E-mail: mail@hppsaude.pt

Emergency telephone numbers:

National Emergency Service	112
Red Cross	21 391 3954
Intoxications & Poison	80 825 0143
Saúde 24	808 24 2424

14. EDUCATION

The Portuguese educational system comprises school education, which includes primary (basic) education, secondary education, and higher education.

The co-ordination of the policy regarding the educational system is entrusted to the Ministry of Education (pre-school, primary and secondary education) and to the Ministry of Science and Higher Education (higher education).

14.1 Pre-School Education

Pre-school education is directed towards children aged between 3 and 6 years (age of entry into primary school), its attendance being optional.

14.2 Primary Education

Primary education is compulsory and free of charge and is aimed at children between the ages of 6 and 15. It lasts 9 years and is divided into 3 cycles: 1st cycle with a four-year duration; 2nd cycle with a two-year duration; and 3rd cycle with a three-year duration. On completion students are given a primary school certificate.

Within the scope of primary education, specialised artistic education in dancing or music may be integrated or articulated with the general education.

14.3 Recurrent Primary Education (Night School)

Students who have not completed their primary education within the standard timeframe (by the age of 15) are offered the possibility of completing it within the scope of recurrent primary education. Recurrent primary education has the same objectives, and awards the same certificate as regular primary education, although adopting study plans and methods that are suited to its particular target group.

In some cases recurrent primary education also offers a component of certified vocational training.

14.4 Secondary Education

Secondary education is mandatory, free of charge and is aimed at students who have completed their primary education and lasts for three years. Regular secondary education is organised into:

- General courses (Sciences, Arts, Economics, Mathematics, Languages and Social Studies) aimed mainly at students wishing to obtain a secondary level education in order to be able to pursue higher education studies;
- Technical courses aimed mainly at students wishing to obtain an intermediate level vocational qualification which will enable them to enter into the employment market.

A secondary education certificate is awarded and, in the case of the technical courses, a level 3 vocational qualification certificate is awarded.

Within the scope of primary and secondary education, religion, civic education, new technologies, artist education in theatre, arts and music are integrated throughout general education courses.

14.5 Specialised Arts Education

Specialised arts education courses are taught within the scope of secondary education. The objective of these courses is to provide artistic education for students who wish to pursue their studies at a higher level, prepare professionals in the areas of the visual arts, dancing and music and promote artistic practices, individually or in a group.

14.6 Recurrent Secondary Education (Night School)

Those who did not complete their secondary education at the normal age of attendance (by the age of 18) are offered the possibility of completing it within the scope of recurrent secondary education.

Recurrent secondary education has the same objectives, and awards the same certificate, as regular secondary education, although adopting study plans and methods that are suited to its particular target group.

General and technical courses are offered in a variety of fields. The technical courses provide a level 3 vocational qualification, as well as the secondary education certificate.

14.7 Vocational Training

Those who have completed their primary education are offered professional courses which fall within the specific scope of vocational training.

The professional courses are aimed at preparing individuals to carry out a professional activity, and grant a level 3 vocational qualification certificate, as well as a certificate equivalent to that of secondary education.

These courses have an average duration of 3 years and are held at vocational schools run by the Ministry of Education.

14.8 Post-Secondary Non-Higher Education

Within the special scope of vocational training, there are post-secondary non-higher education courses called technical specialisation courses, aimed predominantly at those who, having acquired a secondary education certificate and a level 3 vocational qualification, wish to further develop their scientific and technical knowledge in the field of their basic vocational training and to develop personal and professional skills suited to a qualified professional practice.

These courses have an overall duration of 1200 to 1560 hours, including 360 to 720 hours of in-house training. On completing these courses a technical specialisation certificate is awarded, granting a level 4 vocational qualification.

14.9 Higher Education

Depending on the nature of the education, higher education comprises university and polytechnic education.

14.10 Access

Access to higher education is subject to "numerus clausus" (limited places) and its admission is determined in accordance with certain entrance requirements. Students holding a secondary education certificate or equivalent, and complying with the requirements fixed by law, may be admitted to higher education studies. These requirements include examinations in certain subject matters and the achievement of certain minimum scores therein.

14.11 University Education

Within the scope of university education the following degrees are awarded:

(i) Graduate (*licenciatura*), through courses with a four or five-year duration;
(ii) Masters, through a process with a total duration of two years, which includes a specialisation course and the elaboration and defence of a dissertation. Only graduates may be admitted to a master's course;
(iii) Doctorate, through the elaboration and defence of a thesis. Only individuals possessing a masters degree, and under certain conditions graduates, are granted access to study a doctoral degree.

This education is provided by universities which are organised, according to the terms established by their statutes, into units that may adopt various designations; for example, faculty, institute, school, and department. University education may also be provided in university schools, which are not integrated into universities and are normally of a specialised nature.

14.12 Polytechnic Education

Within the scope of polytechnic education the following degrees are awarded:

(i) Bachelors, through courses with a three-year duration;

(ii) Graduate, through courses with a three or four year duration.

This education is provided in polytechnic institutes which are organised, according to the terms established by their statutes, into specialised units normally called higher education schools or colleges.

Polytechnic education may also be provided in schools which are not integrated into polytechnic institutes, also of a specialised nature.

More detailed information on the Portuguese educational system may be obtained from the services of the Ministry of Education and the Ministry of Science and Higher Education:

www.mctes.pt
www.min-edu.pt

International Schools in Portugal:

Lisbon Area

Boa Ventura Montessori Nursery School

Address: Rua Nunes dos Santos, 5, 2765-546 São Pedro do Estoril
Tel. (+351) 21 468 80 23
Fax (+351) 21 468 80 23
Website: boaventuramontessori.com
E-mail: info@boaventuramontessori.com

Carlucci American International School of Lisbon

Address: Rua António dos Reis 95, Linhó 2710-301 Sintra
Tel. (+351) 21 923 98 00
Fax (+351) 21 923 98 09
Website: www.caislisbon.org
E-mail: info@caislisbon.org

Cascais International School

Address: Rua das Faias, Lote 7, Torre, 2750-688 Cascais
Tel. (+351) 21 484 62 60

International Preparatory School

Address: Rua do Boror, 12, 2775-557 Carcavelos
Tel. (+351) 214 570 149
Fax (+351) 214 573 501
Website: www.ipsschool.org
E-mail: info@ipsschool.org

Montessori International School

Address: Estrada de Oeiras, 22, Porto Salvo, 2780-284 Oeiras
Tel. (+351) 21 421 28 48

St. Dominic's International School

Address: Rua Maria Brown, 2785-816 S. Domingos de Rana
Tel. (+351) 21 444 0434 / 351 21 448 0550
Fax (+351) 21 444 3072
Website: dominics-int.org
E-mail: school@dominics-int.org

St. Julian's School

Address: Quinta Nova, 2776-601 Carcavelos
Tel. (+351) 21 458 53 00
Fax (+351) 21 458 53 13
Website: www.stjulians.com
E-mail:mail@stjulians.com

St. Peter's School

Address: Quinta dos Barreleiros, CCI 395, Volta da Pedra, 2950-201 Palmela
Tel. (+351) 21 233 6990
Fax (+351) 21 233 6999
Website: www.st-peters-school.com

Queen Elizabeth's School

Address: Rua Filipe de Magalhães nº 1, 1700-194 Lisboa
Tel. (+351) 21 841 01 40
Fax (+351) 21 841 0149
Website: www.qes.pt
E-mail: info@qes.pt / info.qes@gmail.com

Oporto Area

Colégio Luso Internacional de Braga

Address: Rua da Igreja Velha, Gualtar, 4710-069 Braga
Tel. (+351) 25 367 98 60
Fax (+351) 25 367 98 62
Website: www.clib.pt
E-mail: secretaria@clib.pt

Colégio Luso Internacional do Porto

Address: Rua de Vila Nova, 1071, 4100-506 Porto
Tel. (+351) 22 619 91 60
Fax (+351) 22 619 91 60
Website: www.clip.pt
E-mail: info@clip.pt

Oporto British School

Address: Rua da Cerca, 326/350, 4150-201 Porto
Tel. (+351) 22 616 66 60
Website: www.obs.edu.pt
E-mail: school@obs.edu.pt

Algarve Area

Barlavento International English School Algarve

Address: Caixa 250-Z Ferrel – Espiche, 8600-110 Lagos
Tel. (+351) 28 278 92 06
Website: www.internationalprimaryschoolalgarve.com
E-mail: info@internationalschoolalgarve.com

International School of Algarve

Address: Apartado 80, Porches, 8400-400 Lagoa
Tel. (+351) 28 234 25 47
Fax (+351) 28 235 37 87
Website: www.internationalschoolofthealgarve.com
E-mail: geral@eialgarve.com

International School São Lourenço

Address: Sítio da Rabona, 8135 Almancil
Tel. (+351) 28 939 83 28
Fax (+351) 28 939 82 98
Website: algarveschool.com
E-mail: info@algarveschool.com

Vale Verde International School

Address: Apartado 125, Luz, 8601-927 Lagos
Tel. (+351) 28 269 72 05
Fax (+351) 28 247 17 61
Website: www.vvis.org

Vilamoura International School

Address: Apartado 856, 8125-911 Vilamoura
Tel. (+351) 28 930 32 80
Fax (+351) 28 930 32 88

Madeira

Madeira British School

Address: Caminho dos Saltos 6, 9050-219 Funchal
Tel. (+351) 29 177 32 18
Fax (+351) 29 175 72 06
Website: www.britishschoolmadeira.com
E-mail: principal@britishschoolmadeira.com

International School of Madeira

Address: Calçada do Pico nº5, 9000-206 Funchal
Tel. (+351) 29 122 58 70
Website: www.madeira-international-school.com
E-mail: info@madeira-international-school.com

15. DEATH

Cremation is legal in Portugal but there are only three crematoriums: one at the *Cemitério do Alto de São João* in Lisbon, one at the *Cemitério do Prado do Repouso* in Oporto and the other at the *Cemitério de Ferreira do Alentejo* in the small town of Ferreira do Alentejo.

Bodies buried at municipal cemeteries in Portugal are exhumed after three years when the next-of-kin may arrange to have the remains cremated or transferred to a wall box. If the body is not fully decomposed, it will be buried again for further periods of 2 years until decomposition is complete.

Due to the very great shortage of space, the British Cemetery in Lisbon is reserved for the burial of Protestants residing in Portugal whose normal place of worship is St George's Church, Lisbon, St Paul's Church, Estoril, St Vicente's Church, Portimão or St Andrew's Church of Scotland.

Transportation of a body or ashes to the UK should be handled by a reputable firm of undertakers.

16. BRITISH INSTITUTIONS

There are numerous British and international organisations in Portugal, some of which are as follows:

Clubs and Societies

Lisbon Casuals Sports Club
Royal British Legion
St Andrew's Society
The Royal Society of St George
St David's Society
The Women's Royal Voluntary Service
The British Historical Society of Portugal
The Lisbon Players (theatrical group)
The Royal British Club

For further information on the British community, the British Community Council's website may be consulted at www.bcclisbon.org.

The British Council maintains offices in Lisbon, Coimbra, Oporto, Almada, Cascais, Alverca and Queluz. It organises many educational and cultural events and has a lending and reference library and an excellent information service.

17. ENGLISH LANGUAGE NEWSPAPERS

The Algarve Resident is an English newspaper. Further information can be found on: www.algarveresident.com, The News (www.theportugalnews.com) is published weekly, and is widely read by the international community. Both carry a classified ads section.

The Madeira Island Bulletin (www.madeiraisland.com), is published monthly and specialises in information of particular interest to those living in Madeira.

18. LANGUAGE

English is spoken in the main commercial and tourist centres but some knowledge of Portuguese is essential for those wishing to settle in this country. It would not be possible to find permanent employment without the ability to communicate in Portuguese. There are many language schools that teach Portuguese as a foreign language, and individual tuition is also readily available.

19. FURTHER HELP AND ADVICE

There are a number of relocation agencies in Portugal who, for a fee, will provide assistance in negotiating maze of Portuguese bureaucracy.

However, AFPOP - the Association of Foreign Property Owners in Portugal - is a non-profit organisation, founded in 1987 with the objective of assisting foreign property owners overcome difficulties in the Portuguese real estate market. Today, the Association covers a much wider range of services and activities. It is directed and administered by a management council and area delegates who have many collective years of experience of living in Portugal. It operates from an office in Portimão offering members full time service and advice. For details of membership, contact AFPOP, Apartado 728, 8501-917 Portimão, Tel 282 458 509, Fax 282 458 277, e-mail members@afpop.com

20. CONSULAR REGISTRATION

Consular registration, though not mandatory in Portugal, is important as it enables the British Embassy to assist British residents more efficiently when certificates are required, and to contact residents speedily, if necessary.

Consular registration cards may be obtained from any of the following offices:

British Embassy

Consular Section

Address: Rua de São Bernardo, 33, 1249-082 Lisboa
After-hours Service: (+351) 28 249 07 50
Tel. (+351) 21 392 40 00
Fax (+351) 21 392 41 53
E-mail: Lisbon.Consulate@fco.gov.uk

Porto British Consulate

Address: Travessa Barão de Forrester, 86, 4400 - 034 Vila Nova de Gaia
Tel. (+351) 22 618 4789
Fax (+351) 22 610 0438
E-mail: britcon.oporto@sapo.pt

Algarve British Consulate

Address: Edificio A Fabrica, Avenida Guanaré, 8501-915 Portimão
Tel. (+351) 28 249 07 50
Fax (+351) 28 241 40 54
E-mail: bc.portimao@netcabo.pt

Madeira Honorary British Consulate

Address: Rua da Alfândega, 10, 3C, Funchal
Tel. (+351) 29 121 28 60
Fax (+351) 29 121 28 69
E-mail: Britcon.Funchal@NetMadeira.com

Azores Honorary British Consulate

Address: Largo Vasco Bensaude, 13, 9500 - 234 Ponta Delgada, S. Miguel , Açores
Tel. (+351) 29 662 81 92
Fax (+351) 29 662 81 75

More information can be obtained at the British Embassy's Website: **ukinportugal.fco.gov.uk/pt**

21. WORKING IN PORTUGAL

21.1. Free Movement of Workers

As aforementioned in Section 2, EU Nationals are permitted to travel, circulate and work freely in any Member State, enjoying the same rights as the citizens of a host Member State. Family members are also entitled to free circulation, irrespective of their nationality.

Consequently EU Nationals have the right to carry out a professional activity in Portugal, under either an employed or self-employed regime, without the need to apply for a work permit. They also have the same rights as Portuguese workers with regards to salary, working conditions, access to lodging, vocational training, social assistance and trade union rights.

EU Nationals may enter and circulate in Portugal without the necessity to comply with any formality. All that is required is the possession of a valid identificatory document (passport or identity card). Nevertheless, where the intention is to stay in Portugal for more than 3 months it is advisable to apply for a Residence Card in order to certify your situation as an EU National.

21.2 Residence Permit

More detailed information can be found in Section 2 above.

21.3 Social Assistance

The Social Assistance System in Portugal is managed by the Institute of Solidarity and Social Assistance.

The system consists of the General Contributory Scheme which covers employees, self-employed workers and their respective dependents and the

Non-Contributory Scheme which grants social protection to people with economic or social needs not covered by the general scheme.

21.4 Employment accidents

The social assistance system does not cover accidents at work. This type of protection is, as a rule, provided by means of an insurer hired by the company where the employee carries out his professional activity.

Self-employed workers should take out an individual contract with an insurance company if they wish to be protected against employment-related accidents.

21.5 Registering under the General Social Assistance Scheme

Workers may only receive social assistance payments if they are registered with the Regional Social Assistance Centre covering the area in which they work.

Employers are obliged to register their employees under the general social assistance scheme up until the end of the month following the one in which they started working. Nevertheless within 24 hours of starting the employment the employee must also advise the Regional Social Assistance Centre.

Workers wishing to pursue a professional activity under a self-employed scheme in Portugal should inform the tax authorities in the area where they set up their residence, of the date on which they started their professional activity and should register under the general social assistance schemes for self-employed workers.

21.6 Beneficiary's Card

Once registered the worker receives a social assistance beneficiary's card.

21.7 Contributions

The social assistance system is financed by the contributions paid by the employer and the employee. The contribution is calculated by applying an overall rate of 34.75% to the employees' gross salary: 11% is deducted monthly from the employees' salary and 23.75% is contributed by the employer. The employer is responsible for making the contribution for each employee at the Regional Social Assistance Centre.

21.8 Self-employed workers

The contribution rate for self-employed workers is calculated on the basis of the salary declared at the Regional Social Assistance Centre, corresponding to 25.4% (for the compulsory protection scheme) or 32% (if the employee chooses the wider protection scheme). The Portuguese Social Security does not, in any case, protect self-employed individuals in the event of unemployment and their compulsory protection scheme does not comprise of social assistance in case of sickness.

21.9 Social Benefits

The general social assistance scheme for employees ensures protection in the following situations:

(i) Sickness

Sickness benefit is paid to an employee in the case of temporary incapacity (sick leave), certified by the competent health services. The Temporary Incapacity Certificate (CIT) must be delivered within 5 working days, by the employee to the Regional Social Assistance Centre where he/she is registered.

The temporary incapacity certificate must be delivered by the employee to the Regional Social Assistance Centre where he/she is registered.

In order to receive sickness benefit the employee must have a record of 6 months' remuneration and must, in the 4 months preceding the sickness, have worked and made deductions during a minimum of 12 days.

Sickness benefit is calculated by the application of a percentage to the beneficiary's remuneration, depending on the duration and nature of the sickness and the benefit cannot be received for over 1095 days for employees or 365 days for self-employed under a wider protection scheme.

Further information should be sought from the nearest Regional Social Assistance Centre.

(ii) Unemployment

The unemployment protection system consists of: unemployment benefit, social unemployment benefit and partial unemployment benefit. The benefits are aimed at compensating the loss of remuneration due to involuntary unemployment and at promoting job creation. The benefits are paid to unemployed individuals residing in Portugal who:

- Find themselves involuntary unemployed;
- Are registered for a new job in the Job Centre of their area of residence.

(a) **Unemployment Benefit.** Beneficiaries must have worked for at least 450 days, with a record of contributions in the 24 months preceding the date of unemployment.

The duration of the unemployment benefit depends on the age of the beneficiary, with a maximum of 360 days (for individuals aged less than 30), 540 days (for individuals aged over 30 and less than 40), 720 days (for individuals aged over 40 and less than 44) and a maximum of 900 months (for individuals aged 45 or over).

The amount of the benefit is 65% of the remuneration reference, and it is calculated on the basis of 30 days a month, with a maximum limit of 3 times the Indexation Mechanism of Social Benefits (*IAS*).

(b) **Unemployment Social Benefit** is paid to all beneficiaries who worked for 180 days, with a record of contributions in the 12 months preceding the date of unemployment and whose family income is lower than 80% per person of the national minimum wage. The duration of social benefit is identical to that established for unemployment benefit. The amount of this benefit is equal to the *IAS* for beneficiaries with a family and 80% of the national minimum wage for individual beneficiaries.

(c) **Partial Unemployment Benefit** is paid when the beneficiary who is receiving unemployment benefit and signs a part-time employment contract, with remuneration lower than the amount provided in unemployment benefit.

(iii) Transfer of Unemployment Benefit

Where an individual receiving unemployment benefit in his/her home country wishes to seek employment in Portugal, it possible to make an application for the unemployment benefits to be transferred to Portugal for a maximum period of 3 months. Nevertheless, the following rules should be observed with respect to the home country: the applicant must remain available for employment in the respective Public Employment Service for a minimum period of 4 weeks, inform the competent Social Assistance entity of the intention to seek employment in Portugal, indicate the departure date, and register for employment with the Public Employment Service in Portugal (IEFP), within the 7 days immediately following departure.

It will be necessary to present an E303 form which may be obtained from the competent Social Security entity in the home country. It will also be advisable to obtain an E301 form.

In Portugal the general social assistance scheme further contemplates the following types of protection: maternity, paternity and adoption; family responsibilities; professional risks; disability, old age and death.

To obtain more information on all entitlements to social assistance benefits while working in Portugal, it is advisable to contact the Regional Social Assistance Centre in your area of residence: www.seg-social.pt.

21.10 Seeking Employment

It will not be easy to find a job without at least some knowledge of the Portuguese language. As a reminder, EU Nationals do not require a work permit and are entitled to the same employment opportunities as Portuguese citizens.

Before deciding to travel to Portugal to look for a job it is advisable to contact the EURES Network services in the country of origin. A EURES Advisor will be able to provide current information on the labour market in Portugal.

Information on the EURES Network may be viewed at: www.europa.eu.int/eures. Here they provide details concerning offers of employment and on the living and working conditions in Portugal or in any other EEA country.

Individuals already in Portugal may look for a job in:

- **Job Centres**

The Public Employment Service (*IEFP - Instituto de Emprego e Formação Profissional*) has a network of job centres. Registration as a job seeker may be carried out at the job centre closest to the area of residence and information requested concerning job vacancies throughout the country. In order to register a valid personal identification document or passport will be required and a document attesting the job seeker's right of permanent residence in Portugal.

Addresses of the IEFP's job centres may be consulted at www.iefp.pt. This site also grants access to offers of employment and it may be possible to register for a job online.

As a reminder, where unemployment benefit has been transferred to Portugal it is mandatory to register as a job seeker at a job centre within 7 days of leaving the country of origin.

The job centre will provide the address of the Regional Social Assistance Centre in order to complete the process and submit an E303 form.

- **Temporary Work Agencies**

An application may also be made for a job at temporary employment agencies which assign registered individuals to other companies. Accepting temporary employment may be a means of finding and securing a regular job.

The addresses of authorised Temporary Work Agencies may be accessed at: www.iefp.pt.

- **The Press**

Portuguese companies make frequent use of national and regional newspapers to advertise their job vacancies.

The internet may be consulted for employment opportunities advertised in the Portuguese newspapers most frequently used by employers: *Diário de Noticias*classificados.lojadojornal.pt;*Público:*www.classificados.publico.clix. pt;and *Correio da Manhã* - (www.empregosonline.pt) publish job offers in a variety of activity sectors, daily. The weekly newspaper *Expresso* (www.aeiou.expressoemprego.pt) publishes a booklet with job offers aimed at qualified experts, executives and consultants.

- **Professional Associations, Chambers of Commerce & Industry and Trade Unions.**

These are also information sources available in order to assess the job opportunities in Portugal.

21.11 Employment Legal Framework

As aforementioned, EU Nationals have the same rights regarding salary, working conditions, social assistance, and trade union membership as Portuguese citizens.

21.11.1 Employment Contracts

In Portugal only citizens over the age of 16 and with the compulsory level of schooling (12th grade) may enter into an employment contract. Before signing a contract it is advisable to consider its terms and conditions carefully and ensure that its contents are fully understood, if necessary by having it translated into English.

(i) Type of Employment Contract:

According to the applicable legal provisions, fixed term or non-fixed term employment contracts must be made in writing, while on the other hand this is optional for indefinite term (permanent) employment contracts.

(a) **A fixed or non-fixed term contract** may be entered into in the following cases: temporary substitution of an employee; seasonal activities; civil construction, public works, industrial assembly and repair activities under a regime of direct piecework; and development of projects that are not part of the employer's current activity.

(b) **A fixed term contract** is also possible in cases of: temporary or exceptional growth of the activity; execution of a specific precisely defined and non-permanent occasional task or service; launch of a new activity of uncertain duration or start-up of the company or establishment; hiring employees seeking their first job or long-term unemployed individuals.

A fixed-term contract that cannot be justified in line with the aforesaid requirements will be converted into an indefinite term employment contract.

Fixed term contracts may last for less than 6 months in the following cases: temporary replacement of an employee, seasonal work, temporary or unusual increases in business activity, and occasional task or temporary specific service. In the last two situations, the contracts cannot be entered into for a period shorter than the one estimated for the task or service to be accomplished.

A fixed term employment contract can be renewed up to three times, but their duration, including the renewals shall not exceed:

18 months - in the case of an employee seeking his/her first job;
24 months-if an employer is launching a new activity, starting up a company or hiring long-term unemployed individuals;
36 months – in all other circumstances

If it exceeds these limits, it is automatically converted into an employment contract for an indefinite period.

(ii) Probationary period

For fixed and non-fixed term contracts, the probationary period is of 15 days for contracts with duration of no less than 6 months and 30 days for contracts equal to or greater than 6 months.

For permanent contracts the probationary period varies as follows: 90 days in most circumstances; 180 days for positions of technical complexity, a high degree of responsibility or functions of trust; and up to 240 days for senior staff and managers.

If the probationary period lasts for more than 60 days, the employer must give a minimum of 7 days notice to terminate the contract.

(iii) Employment Hours

The upper limit is 40 hours a week, with no more than 8 hours a day. Overtime may not exceed 200 hours a year and entitles the employee to special remuneration and time off.

The mandatory weekly period of rest is 1 day. Work performed on the day of rest entitles the worker to receive double the remuneration and 1 remunerated day off.

(iv) Vacations

For fixed and non-fixed term contracts with duration of greater than 1 year, employees are entitled to a fully paid vacation period of 22 working days (which may be increased by an additional period of three extra days in line with a minimal or non-existent level of absence during the preceding working year) during which time they receive an additional month of salary.

For contracts whose term is less than 6 months or if the employment contract has lasted for less than a year, the vacation period is equal to 2 working days per complete month of work.

There are 12 national holidays and 2 optional holidays.

(v) Salaries

In Portugal there is a national minimum wage, fixed annually by the government. The minimum wage established for 2010 is 475.00 euros.

There are also contractual salaries, negotiated by the union or representative body for each professional group or category, and subsequently defined in collective contracts or agreements that govern the respective industrial or commercial sectors.

Besides the regular monthly remuneration, employees also receive holiday and Christmas subsidies, bringing the total to 14 months of salary per year.

For further information on employment legislation and the rights of employees, it is advisable to contact:

21.11.2 Recognition of Vocational Training Certificates and Diplomas

In Portugal as in the other Member States, access to certain professional activities is conditional on a minimum level of qualification having been attained, whether certificate, diploma, or higher degree.

In these circumstances, recognition of the vocational qualification to carry out a profession is achieved through a qualification recognition system, established among the Member States.

This system is applicable to individuals who are qualified to carry out a profession in one Member State and who wish to carry out the same profession in another Member State where this profession is regulated. Consequently if the profession in question is regulated in Portugal, recognition of foreign qualifications should be obtained locally before being able to carry out the profession.

The professions which are regulated in Portugal are, among others: lawyers, chartered accountants, general practitioners and specialists, nurses responsible for general health care, dentists, midwives, veterinarians, pharmacists, psychologists, architects, engineers, industrial property agents, navy officials and secondary school teachers. Besides these, a further set of professional activities is also regulated, such as: hairdressing, personal services and transportation.

Where the profession in question is not regulated in Portugal, it is not necessary to request the recognition of foreign professional qualifications; professional activity may be carried out under the same conditions as Portuguese citizens.

(i) Recognition mechanism

Recognition is given to the diplomas, certificates, degrees or set of degrees that sanction a complete vocational training, that is, that enable the profession in question to be carried out in the home member state. As a rule, a diploma, certificate or degree should be recognised as such.

The recognition system is not automatic. Recognition must be applied for at the competent authority which will examine each case individually, ensuring that:

(a) The regulated profession to be carried out is the one for which the individual is fully qualified in the Member State of origin; and

(b) The duration and content of training do not differ significantly from those that are locally required. If the professions are the same and the respective training is similar overall, the competent authority should recognise the foreign qualifications. On the other hand, where there are substantial differences between the professions or between the length and content of the respective training, a compensatory measure may be imposed.

(ii) Compensatory measures

Where there is a difference of at least 1 year in the duration of the training, the competent authority may require the acquisition of professional experience (the extent of which may range from 1 to 4 years).

Where there are considerable differences in terms of the professions themselves or of the content of the training, it may be mandatory (as a rule, at the individual's choice) to undergo a training period or an examination. In any case, only one compensatory measure may be imposed.

In addition, professional experience that may have been acquired should be taken into account, which may reduce, or even do away with, the compensatory measure envisaged.

(iii) Special cases

(a) If the profession in relation to which recognition of qualifications has been recognised is not regulated in the individual's home country, the competent Portuguese authority may require 2 years' professional experience.

(b) If the diploma was obtained in a country which falls outside the EEA (European Economic Area) but has already been recognised in one Member State, and the profession in question has been carried out in that Member State for 2 or 3 years, it may be recognised in Portugal.

(iv) Information on formalities in Portugal

Applications for recognition should be directed to the competent authority in Portugal for receiving and analysing the requests regarding the regulated profession in question. To identify the competent authority in any specific case, contact:

NARIC
Ministério da Educação
Departamento do Ensino Superior - Núcleo Pedagógico
Av. Duque de Ávila, 137-4°
1050 Lisboa
www.naricportugal.pt

Where the profession is unregulated, it may become necessary to request professional equivalence. This process involves the recognition and certification of the professional skills of workers who obtained their qualification in another member state and which grants them access to specific professions that require a Portuguese degree.

These requests should be directed to:

Instituto do Emprego e Formação Profissional
Departamento de Certificação
Rua de Xabregas, 52
1949-003 Lisbon
www.iefp.pt

(v) Documentation to be submitted together with a request

To obtain a list of the exact documents that must be presented, the competent authority should be contacted. The documents that will, most likely, be necessary to present are the following: a nationality certificate of a member state; an authenticated copy of the diplomas or degrees obtained; in some cases a medical certificate and/or proof of a clean criminal record.

Furthermore if the profession in question is not regulated in an individual's home member state, a certificate should be presented stating that the profession has been carried out for at least two of the previous 10 years.

(vi) Translations

In some cases it will be necessary to present a translation into Portuguese of these documents. This translation should be obtained, at the individual's own expense, from a sworn translator or a Portuguese diplomatic or consular authority in the home country.

The administrative decision should be taken no later than three months from the date on which the completed dossier was submitted. The interested party has the right to an appeal in the case of a negative decision.

CHECK LIST

Before accepting a job, possession of the following documents should be ensured:

- Valid identity document or passport.
- Employment contract or document confirming the conditions offered, fully understood.
- Details concerning the method and frequency of the salary to be received.
- E111 form or health insurance so as to safeguard against possible health expenses.

It is also advisable to:

- Try and obtain the most important Portuguese newspapers, in order to check the employment market situation.
- Ensure contacts in the home country which may serve as a reference to future employers in Portugal.
- Ensure at least some knowledge of the Portuguese language.

22. TAXES ON INCOME AND VAT

22.1 Taxes on Income

Taxpayers in Portugal must apply for a Fiscal Identification Number (*Número de Identificação Fiscal* - NIF) at their local tax office (*Serviço de Finanças*). This fiscal identification number is also necessary for opening a bank account, entering into a long-term rental agreement, purchasing property and obtaining a road tax.

(i) Individual Income Tax (*Imposto sobre o Rendimento das Pessoas Singulares* - IRS)

Individual Income Tax is due on the worldwide income received by individuals residing in Portugal as well as on the income received or deemed to have been received in Portugal by non-resident individuals.

In a family unit, tax is levied on the total amount of income received by the persons who are part thereof. A couple living together with any dependent children are taxed jointly as a family. Consequently, a single tax return is submitted to the tax authority.

For tax purposes, civil partners can opt to be treated as married couples. Therefore the tax rules applicable to married couples can equally apply to civil partners from the beginning of the partnership.

The term dependant means :

(i) an adopted child or stepchild if minor of age;

(ii) a minor under legal guardianship;

(iii) an adult under the age of 25 whose yearly income is higher than the national minimum wage;

(iv) an adult under the age of 25 who is incapacitated for work ;

(v) an adult under the age of 25 who is unable to support himself/herself financially.

A Dependant may be taxed as a separate family unit..

- **Concept of Residence (IRS Code)**

The following individuals are deemed to be resident in Portugal with respect to the year in which the taxable income was obtained:

(a) Individuals who spend more than 183 days (6 months) consecutively or non-consecutively in Portugal or remain for a lesser period but maintain residence on December 31st of the same year that demonstrates the intention of maintaining a regular domicile therein.

(b) Individuals who, although being abroad, are employed by the Portuguese State exercising a public function or commission in the service thereof.

(c) Members of the same family unit if the responsible member of the family is a Portuguese resident.

Residents in Portugal who receive foreign-source income are entitled to a tax credit equal to the lower of the foreign tax paid or the Portuguese tax payable on such income, and is limited to the amount of tax payable in the country of source.

- Concept of Income deemed to have been received in Portugal

The following categories of income are deemed to have been received in Portugal:

(a) Income arising from activities performed therein;

(b) Labour earnings arising from activities carried out in Portugal, or those paid by a resident entity;

(c) Income arising from directors remuneration, paid by a resident company;

(d) Income arising from employment abroad an aircraft or a vessel, if the employer is a resident entity.

(e) Income arising from payments made by an entity residing, or with head offices, place of management or permanent establishment, in Portugal in respect of:

-Intellectual or industrial property rights;

-The supply of know-how in the commercial, industrial or scientific fields;

-Commercial activities or supply of services arising from a permanent establishment located in Portugal or carried out within this territory, except for services related to transportation, communications or financial activities;

-Intermediation activities;

-Any other capital income;

(f) Income arising from property situated in the Portuguese territory, including capital gains arising from the transfer thereof;

(g) Capital gains resulting from:

-The transfer of shares and securities of resident companies;

-The transfer of industrial or intellectual property rights if the vendor is not the original owner of such rights;

-Derivative financial instruments, if such gains are paid by a resident entity;

(h) Gambling, lotteries or raffle prizes if paid by a resident entity;

(i) Income arising from pensions paid by a resident entity;

(j) Income arising from one-off transactions;

(k) Income arising from activities carried out by artists or sportsmen in Portugal.

- **Tax Assessment**

Tax on individual income is assessed in four steps:

(a) Category-specific tax-deductible expenses are deducted from the gross income received within each category of income listed above, in order to determine taxable income (TI) per category;

(b) Total Taxable Income (TTI) is then determined by adding up all categories of TI;

(c) Tax rates in force are then applied to TTI so as to determine the basic tax assessment (BTI);

(d) Final tax assessment, i.e. amount of income tax payable by taxpayer is determined by deducting from the BTI any pertinent expenses listed in the IRS Code (health and education expenses, tax credits arising from international double taxation, amounts paid by way of tax withheld at source, among others).

Please note that there are two methods of assessing income tax in respect of Income Category B (Business and Supply of Services Activities): the simplified assessment method and the organized accounts method. It would be advisable to consult a tax adviser for comprehensive assessment under this category.

Categories of Taxable Income

Individual Income Tax applies to, and is due in accordance with, the categories of income set out in the following chart:

Categories of income: A - Dependent work (covers all employment-related earnings and certain fringe benefits) B - Business Activities and Supply of Services (covers earnings arising from commercial or industrial activities and/or from the supply of services) E - Capital income (covers remuneration paid by way of interest on capital investments, loans or bank deposits as well as share dividends) F - Property income (covers income arising from property lease or rental)

G - Capital and other gains (covers capital gains, compensation awards and gambling, lotteries or raffle prizes)
H - Pensions (covers retirement and disability pensions)

In Portugal, the taxpayer must submit his own income tax return annually between February 1st and March 15th for earnings derived from salaried employment and/or pensions, and between March 16th and April 30th for all other sources of income. Married couples must submit a combined tax return.

Individual Income Tax due in accordance with the five categories of income set out above is levied at rates varying from 10.5-42% as per tables published annually by the Tax Authorities. Payable Tax is due by May 31st of each year, and overpayments are refunded by August 31st.

Tax assessment on individual income is made in several steps. Category-specific tax-deductible expenses may be deducted from the gross income received within each category of income in order to determine taxable income per category.

Tax deductible expenses are as follows: medical expenses, loans for the acquisition or improvement of a Portuguese residence or rental payments, educational expenses, life insurance and acquisition of stakes in recently privatised companies.

Self-employed individuals, prior to commencing their professional activities, must register for tax purposes at the local tax office and on an annual basis are obliged to make 3 IRS advance payments on account prior to the 20th day of the each of the months of July, September and December.

(ii) Withholding Tax on Individual Income Tax

Employees' payments are subject to withholding tax in accordance with a set of tables published annually by the tax authorities.

Payment to non-residents in relation to the rendering of independent work, supply of services, royalties (if received by the original owner) or technical assistance are subject to a final withholding tax of 20%.

For further information please contact *Ministério das Finanças.*

(iv) Double Taxation Treaty

Portugal has signed a double taxation treaty with the UK and other countries. In accordance with its provisions withholding tax rates on certain types of income can be reduced or exempted. In order to benefit from this reduction or exemption a certificate of residency, as approved by the authorities of the country of residence, must be submitted to the tax authorities where the taxpayer requires the reduction or exemption of payment of tax.

For further information on this double taxation treaty the Inland Revenue website may be consulted at:

www.ir.gov.uk/manuals/DTRmanual/html/DTR15400/17_0064_DT15671.htm.

22.2. VAT

Similarly to the UK, VAT (*IVA - Imposto sobre o Valor Acrescentado*) is a general consumer tax payable by suppliers of goods and services, chargeable on every instance of supply made within the scope of their respective activities, and payable later to the Tax Authorities.

VAT is a tax on consumer expenditure and therefore companies (where they are VAT registered and fully taxable) do not bear the final costs of this tax. They are able to charge VAT on the goods or services they supply (output VAT) and recover VAT on purchases (input VAT).

VAT is levied at the following rates:

Rates	Portugal	Azores and Madeira
Reduced rate	5%	4%
Intermediate rate	12%	8%
General rate	20%	14%

Building contracts are taxable at a rate of 21%.

For further information:

www.min-financas.pt
www.dgci.min-financas.pt/siteinternet/index.html
www.infocid.pt

23. HOUSING, ACCOMMODATION AND RENTS

Accommodation is expensive, particularly in and around Lisbon, Oporto and Funchal. Long term rentals in the Algarve are difficult to find and, if available, are often very expensive. Locating suitable accommodation can be a time-consuming process.

Hotels are subject to Government control. *Pousadas* (historic hotels) range from reasonable to expensive. Hotel lists are available in the Portuguese National Tourist Office, most travel agents or via the internet.

23.1. How to Find a Place to Stay

When hired to work in Portugal, assistance may be requested from the employer to help with finding a place to stay. The following sources of information may also prove useful:

- **The Newspapers**

Houses/apartments that are to let or for sale are advertised either directly by the owners or through Real Estate Agencies in the national, regional and local newspapers such as *O Público*, *Diário de Notícias*, *Correio da Manhã* and *Jornal de Notícias*. The weekly newspaper *Expresso* has a separate booklet with advertisements for lodging.

For further information:

Diário de Notícias: classificados.lojadojornal.pt;
Público: classificados.publico.clix.pt;
Correio da Manhã: www.imobiliariocm.pt;
Sol: www.imobiliario.sol.pt;

- **Real Estate Agencies**

Houses/apartments that are to let or are for sale may have a sign saying *vende-se* (for sale) or *arrenda-se* (to let), with a telephone number or address for direct contact and or to request information. The contact may be the owner or a real estate agency.

23.2. Types of Lodging

(i) Rented Housing

The offer of houses/apartments to rent is very limited. In the big cities an apartment with 1-2 bedrooms may cost approximately 500 - 1,000 euros per month. Non-furnished apartments are not necessarily cheaper than furnished ones.

(a) The Lease Agreement

The key clauses of a lease agreement are the identification of the parties, the property to be leased, specification of the rent and its due date.

Non-stipulation in writing of any other elements of the lease agreement will not affect its validity and effectiveness. Legal provisions on lease agreements will then apply.

(b) Sub-letting

The lessee cannot sub-let the property without express consent in writing by the lessor. Sub-letting agreements terminate upon expiry of the main lease agreement. Nevertheless, if the main lease agreement terminates due to the death of the principal lessee, the sub-lessee will not have the right to sign a new lease agreement.

(c) Duration and Termination of the Lease Agreement

Fixed term lease agreements are the most common types of lease agreements in Portugal.

These agreements have to be entered into for a minimum of a 5 years period and its duration must unequivocally be determined in its clauses. The assignment of contractual rights does not entail either the suspension or the interruption of this period.

The termination of lease agreements occurs in any the following circumstances:

- *By notice:* Notice may be given by the lessor, through judicial summons, 1 year prior to the expiry date of the fixed term of the agreement. A lessee who wishes to end the lease agreement must do so through a written declaration addressed to the lessor, at least 120 days before the date of its expiry, with effect 30 days following notification.

If no notice is given within the aforementioned period, the lease agreement will automatically be renewed for another 3 years.

- *By mutual consent:* Parties may, at any time, revoke the lease agreement by mutual agreement.

- *By expiration:* The lease agreement will expire in any of the following circumstances:

- When the rental period agreed on by the parties or stipulated by law comes to an end;
- If the lease agreement entails a condition precedent (suspensive condition), it is suspended until a specific event has taken place or if

it is subject to a condition subsequent (resolutory condition) it will be terminated when the condition is fulfilled;

- When the right (e.g. usufruct) or managing powers of the lessor terminate. In this situation, the lessee has no right to enter into a new lease agreement;
- Upon death of the lessee or in the case of a corporate entity, where it has been wound up;
- With the loss of the property;
- With termination of the services which effected the lease agreement;
- When the property is the object of expropriation, unless the lease agreement is compatible with the same.

- *By rescission:* A breach of contract by the lessee may give the right to rescission by the lessor in any of the following circumstances:

If the lessee:

- Does not pay the rent on the due date (3 months delay);
- Uses, or allows someone else to use, the property for a purpose other than the one agreed;
- Uses the property for unlawful, indecent or dishonest practices;
- Carries out construction works that substantially alter the structure of the property or the internal disposition of its divisions that cannot be considered as being for the purposes of the lessee's own comfort;
- Provides lodging, sublets or loans the property, wholly or in part, without the lessor's prior permission;
- Collects from the sub-lessee an unlawful rent;
- Does not live in the property for a year, except in situations of *force majeur*, or of prolonged absence due to disease or exercise of public functions;
- Opposes the carrying out of works ordered by a public authority.

The eviction claim must be filed within one year following knowledge of the events that give grounds to the eviction claim.

(d) Rent and Rent Increase

The rent must be settled in euros, of a fixed value and the rent clause must foresee the form and terms in which the rent must be paid. This is an essential element of the lease agreement.

If the payment of rent is to be carried out in accordance with the months of the Gregorian calendar, the first rent will be due on signature of the lease agreement and the following on the first working day of the month preceding the one to which it refers.

Failure to pay rent on the due date or in the following 8 days will put the lessee in breach of the lease agreement. This breach will be remedied if the rent in arrears is paid with an increase of 50% of the amount originally due.

Failure to pay the rent will ultimately bring about eviction proceedings. However, in these circumstances, if the rent is settled in court with the abovementioned additional increase of 50% within the time frame of the counter-pleadings, the eviction claim will be dismissed.

Payment of rent may be made by means of a bank transfer, if expressly agreed beforehand. The bank receipt is equivalent to acquittance.

The rent can be increased:

(i) annually, by application of the coefficient determined yearly by the government;
(ii) annually, by agreement of the parties, where permitted by law;
(iii) as a result of repairs or improvements to the property (this increase is added to the annual increase)

(e) Obligations of the Parties in the Performance of the Lease Agreement

The main obligations of the lessor are to deliver the property to the lessee and to ensure that it allows use for the purpose stipulated in the lease agreement. The lessor has a continuous obligation to permit the use of the property for the purpose stipulated in the lease agreement and may not hinder such use.

The lessee's obligations are the following:

- To pay the agreed rent within the legal timeframe;
- To allow the lessor to exam the property;
- Not to use the property for any purpose different from the one agreed with the lessor;
- To use the property with due diligence;
- To allow repairs to the property, when of an urgent nature or imposed by public authorities;
- Not to provide to any third party the total or partial use of the property, by assignment of contractual rights, sub-letting or loan;
- If previously authorised, inform the lessor of the assignment of contractual rights within fifteen days following assignment;
- To inform the lessor of any important facts relating to the property;
- To return the leased property, upon termination of the lease agreement, in the same conditions in which it was received from the lessor, with the exception of normal "wear and tear" through reasonable use of the property.

A party will be deemed to be in breach of the lease agreement whenever it fails to comply with any of the abovementioned obligations pursuant to the lease agreement, or its deficient fulfilment.

(ii) Short-term Lodging

If seeking temporary lodging in hotels or boarding houses information may be obtained or a reservation made at the Tourist Offices or on the Internet.

Youth hostels, which charge lower prices, may be an alternative for short-term stays. To qualify for staying at this category of lodging it is necessary to apply for a youth hostel membership card (*cartão de alberguista*) in Portugal. This card is valid for one year from the issue date, and may be obtained at the following places: *movijovem*, youth hostels, regional delegations of the Portuguese Youth Institute or *Loja do Cidadão* (in Lisbon and Oporto).

www.pousadasjuventude.pt

Reservation Office
Tel: +351 707 20 30 30
Fax: + 351 21 723 21 02
E-mail: reservas@movijovem.pt

Loja do Cidadão
Tel: +351 808 241 107
E-mail: lojadocidadao@lojadocidadao.pt

For further information

Portuguese National Tourist Office UK
Address: 11, Belgrave Square, London, SW1X 8PP
UK brochure line: 0845 355 1212
Fax: 020 7201 6633
E-mail: tourism@portugaloffice.org.uk
Web: www.visitportugal.com

(iii) Time-sharing

Although inspired by Anglo-Saxon "time-sharing" features, the use of properties on a time-share basis is addressed differently in Portugal.

The Portuguese legal framework for the use of properties on a timeshare basis is twofold. In fact, time-share utilisation of properties encompasses two types of rights with a different legal nature: The Right *in Rem* of Periodic Residence (*Direito Real de Habitação Periódica* - DRHP) and the Right of Touristic Residence (*Direito de Habitação Turística* - DHT). Both rights confer time-shared use of properties, but while the first is a right in rem the other is a straightf orward right of credit.

(a) The Right *In Rem* of Periodic Residence (*Direito Real de Habitação Periódica* - DRHP)

The right *in rem* to use properties on a timeshare basis refers to specific housing units that are part of an apartment-hotel, a tourist village or a tourist apartment.

This right entitles the use of a tourist property during a certain period of time each year, from a minimum of seven to a maximum of thirty consecutive days. This right is usually perpetual and may not be granted for any less than fifteen years counting from the date of the notarial deed, unless the tourist property is still under construction, in which case the period begins when the resort opens to the public.

The contract for the purchase of a DRHP must be made by means of a notarial deed.

For each DRHP, the land registry office issues a certificate granting the right and certifying the transmission of ownership and payment of any taxes due.

The land registry certificate must be drafted in a language familiar to the purchaser and must enclose all relevant information, namely any taxes or charges owed, the maximum capacity of the housing unit and the exact period during which the rights set out in the contract can be exercised.

Any purchaser of a DRHP may rescind the purchase and sale contract without providing a reason, within 10 working days subsequent to the delivery of the abovementioned contract to the same.

The abovementioned right of rescission of the contract conferred to the purchaser of any DRHP cannot be waived.

All DRHP advertising and promotional literature must identify the owner of the tourist property, the owner of the DRHP units, the provisional classification of the tourist property and the planned opening date. DRHPs may not be presented as financial products.

(b) The Right of Tourist Residence (*Direito De Habitação Turística* - DRT)

This right is defined *a contrario*, thus, any rights of residence in tourist accommodation for a given period of time each year that do not constitute right *in rem* to use properties on a timeshare basis are considered right of residence in tourist accommodation.

Contracts relating to the purchase of these rights must be in writing and drafted in a language familiar to the purchaser. Like DRHPs, this right is usually perpetual may not be granted for any less than 3 years counting from the date that the contract comes into force.

As in DRHPs, any purchaser of a DRT may rescind the purchase and sale contract without providing a reason, within 10 working days subsequent to the date of the signature of the contract.

(iv) Buying a house/apartment

It is more convenient to go to a real estate agency in order to buy a house or apartment. Licensed real estate agencies have the official title of *mediador imobiliário* (real estate mediator) or *sociedade de mediação imobiliária* (society of real estate mediation) and are obliged to display the licence number in all of their branches. Before signing any contract with a real estate agency, make sure that it is in fact legalised.

To buy a house/apartment a bank loan may be applied for, with the mortgage of the house/apartment serving as security. The loan conditions vary according to the individual's financial situation, location of the house/apartment and loan repayment terms.

All Portuguese banking institutions may, in principle, grant bank loans. Where the application for a bank loan is made, before the deed is signed the banking institution will request to take out a life insurance policy as additional security on the mortgage in an amount no lower than the amount of the loan.

PART II: BUYING REAL ESTATE IN PORTUGAL

1. INTRODUCTION

Conveyancing is substantially more complex in Portugal than in common law jurisdictions, given the many steps involved in the transfer of the ownership of property through a purchase and sale, as well as in urban construction and land subdivision.

Land Law in Portugal is regulated by the Portuguese Constitution, the Portuguese Civil Code and ancillary Statutory Provisions.

According to the applicable provisions of the Portuguese Civil Code ("PCC"), matters relating to property are governed by the law of the place where the property is located. Issues regarding real estate in Portugal are governed primarily by the PCC. When acquiring property in Portugal foreign individuals and companies are afforded the same rights as Portuguese citizens.

The PCC makes a primary distinction between immovable and movable property.

In Portugal, the right attached to a real estate is classified as *in rem*. *In rem* is a technical term meaning that the right is associated with a particular property rather than a person.

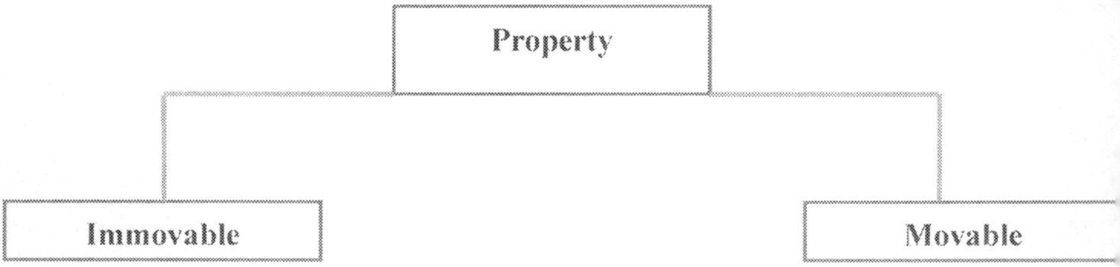

In England and Wales, the system of property ownership is entirely different from that of Portugal and of most Civil Law Jurisdictions.

The English system divides the ownership of real estate property into freehold[1] and leasehold[2] estates. Therefore, leasehold will always be less in duration than freehold and the leaseholder will often be subject to several covenants. The freeholder has an absolute right that endures until his last heir and a much stronger ownership than a leaseholder.

The Portuguese Legal System does not pursue such a division between ownership of property since it does not provide for the concept of leasehold. The owner will always have an absolute right and a tenant will simply be party to a rent/lease agreement.

2. LEGAL FRAMEWORK

The Portuguese key provisions regarding real estate property are contained in:

(i) *The Portuguese Constitution*, Article 62 "Right to private property", which foresees that: *"Every individual shall be guaranteed the right to private property and to the transmission thereof, in life or upon death, as laid down by this Constitution"*;

(ii) *The Portuguese Civil Code*, in particular articles 202 to 216 and articles 1344 to 1384, referring to immovable property;

(iii) *Decree-Laws 384/88* of 25th October and *103/90* of 22nd March, as amended by *Decree-Law 59/91* of 30th January, relating to land consolidation through reparcelling of farmland plots.

(iv) *Decree-Law 281/99* of 26th July, requiring public notaries to verify, before executing a deed of purchase and sale concerning a building or a part

[1] Law Property Act 1925, S1 (1) (a): Fee simple absolute in possession.
[2] Law Property Act 1925, S1 (1) (B): Term of years absolute.

thereof, that a valid construction licence (*Licença de Construção*) or utilisation licence (*Licença de Utilização*) for such a building or part thereof exists or has been applied for;

(v) *Decree-Law 380/99* of 22nd September, as amended by *Decree-Law 53/2000* of 7th April and *Decree-Law 310/2003* of 10th December, establishing the coordination for national, regional and local land management and urban planning;

(vi) *Decree-Law 403/86* of 3rd December, re-enacted by *Decree-Law 533/99* of 11th December and amended by *Decree-laws 273/2001* of 13th October, *323/2001* of 17th December, *38/2003* of 8th March and *8/2007* of 17th January - Land Registration Code (*Código do Registo Predial*).

(vii) *Decree-Law 555/99* of 16th December, as amended by *Decree-Law 177/2001* of 4th June and by *Law 15/2002* of 22nd February, regulating the granting of licences (*Licença Administrativa)* or permits (*Autorização Administrativa*) by the Portuguese Municipalities, for the following activities: construction, modification, restoration and demolition of residential and non-residential buildings or parts, land subdivision, urban planning, subdivision of greenfield sites for purposes of construction.

(viii) *Decree-Law 68/04* of 25th March, laying down the requirements with regard to publicity and information made available to consumers in relation to the purchase of real estate for residential use.

(ix) *Law 6/2006* of 27th February - New Urban Leases Regime - NRAU (*Novo Regime de Arrendamento Urbano*).

3. DEFINITIONS

3.1 Greenfield Sites (*Prédios Rústicos*) and Urban Property (*Prédio Urbano*)

The Portuguese Civil Code differentiates between greenfield sites and urban property. Article 204 (2) thereof defines a greenfield site as a "*confined piece of land, together with any existing associated constructions not having their own economic autonomy"*, and urban property as *"all structures erected on the soil, as well as the land that surrounds the building"*.

Therefore, a given property serves as a greenfield site or as an urban property in accordance with the use it is given by its owner and with State land management and urban planning policies. In particular, such policies are essential in determining whether a greenfield site can be converted into urban property.

Thus, in evaluating a given property, not only its geographical location and size but, also and most especially, land management and urban planning should be taken into consideration.

Furthermore, in accordance with the provisions of Decree-Law 380/99 of 22nd September, referred to above, any member of the public is entitled to access information on land management and urban planning from the State, regional or local authorities, and, as stipulated by Decree-Law 555/99 of 16th December, any interested parties may request, from Municipalities, preliminary information on the feasibility of a given urban development (building construction, demolition or repair and land subdivision). Thus, such authorities are obliged to disclose information about the limitations and restrictions, which may apply to a given property.

3.2 Property Subdivision for Construction Purposes

Subdivision of land for construction purposes is subject to prior authorisation to be granted by the local authority. A licence granted by the City Council (*Câmara Municipal*) or an authorisation granted by the Mayor (*Presidente da Câmara Municipal*) will be required depending on the following circumstances:

(i) A licence granted by the City Council is required where the subdivision relates to one or more properties located in an area not covered by a council-approved development plan (*Plano de Pormenor*);

(ii) An authorisation granted by the Mayor applies wherever such property or properties are located in an area already covered by an approved development plan (*Plano de Pormenor*).

Subdivision licensing procedures may include public discussion of the subdivision project and consultation with external departments (e.g., the Environment Ministry), where legally required. Neither of these procedures is required in subdivision authorisation procedures, as a development plan has already been approved.

Once this licence or authorisation has been granted, the property owner may either submit construction plans or sell the property *en bloc,* together with the benefit of the subdivision licence, or sell each individual plot resulting from the subdivision separately.

3.3 Licence to Build, Modify or Demolish a Building

Construction of a building or modification or demolition thereof can only take place under a licence granted by the City Council or Mayor. However, this licence is not required for modifications to the inside of a building or part thereof, provided that they do not entail any modification to the building's main structure, roofing or façade.

Applications for the licence must include an architectural plan as well as all additional legally required plans, which must be delivered no later than six months following approval of the architectural plan. However, where the application relates to a licence for construction or modification to a building located in an area not covered by a development plan (*Plano de Pormenor*), a partial licence for structural works may be granted upon approval of the architectural plan and delivery of the additional legally required plans.

Where the licence was applied for on behalf of a specific person or entity and this person or entity transfers ownership of the building, or of the property where it is to be built, to a third person, an amendment to the application must be requested, so that the licence can be issued to the new owner.

Upon issue of the licence, supply of utilities such as water, electricity, telephone lines, sewerage amongst others can be applied for.

3.4 Commonhold (*Propriedade Horizontal*[3])

In Portugal, apartments are generally sold under the regime of commonhold. This regime applies to apartments built as independent units with a separate entrance to a common part of the building or directly to the street.

Commonhold is designed to meet the needs of apartment owners and those who own other types of properties which have common parts, i.e. areas which do not belong to any individual unit but are used by all the apartment owners.

In a block of apartments, the common parts are usually ground, roof, entrance hall, stairs, gardens, parking areas and swimming pools.

The developer is responsible for signing a public deed creating the commonhold deed for the whole bloc of apartments and the independent legal deeds for each of the units.

Unit holders will be the exclusive owners of their own apartments and co-owners of the common parts of the building. These two rights may not be sold separately.

The commonhold deed must contain the following elements:

(a) Identification and percentual value of each of the units in relation to the value of the whole building;
(b) The authorised use of each unit (e.g. habitation, commercial purposes);
(c) The condominium regulations (please see below);
(d) Arbitration rules.

The maintenance of the common parts of the building, mandatory fire insurance, security services and other common expenses are paid by the unit holders in accordance with the units' percentage value. A common fund is generally set up to face these expenses.

---

[3] Article 1414 to 1438-A

The condominium regulations must govern the utilisation of the common parts, the maintenance and administration of the building and unit holders' general meetings.

Directors shall be responsible for convening general meetings, administrating the annual condominium budget and accounts, ensuring that the unit holders' contributions are paid on time and the building is adequately insured, and representing the unit holders before local authorities and courts.

Directors, who may be one of the unit holders or a third party, must be elected by the unit holders' general meeting.

Nowadays, professional management companies are widely used to carry out these functions, especially where unit holders are not permanent residents.

4. LEGAL FORMALITIES OF A PURCHASE AND SALE

4.1 Basic Steps: Check List

4.1.1 Buying

BUYING

Obtain Professional Advice

⇩

Obtain copy of entries on the Register

⇩

Negotiate Reservation Agreement/Promissory Contract of Purchase and Sale

⇩

Sign Power of Attorney before a Notary, or at a Portuguese Consulate

⇩

Apply for a fiscal number at local Tax Office

⇩

Obtain tax office certificate from vendor or local Tax Office

⇩

If new property, obtain or ensure vendor obtains a "property passport"

⇩

Transfer deed is signed in the office of a Public Notary

⇩

Register the property in the name of the new owner at local Land Registry

⇩

Update *caderneta predial*

⇩

File *modelo 1* within 60 days

⇩

Verify possession of all documents in respect of transaction

⇩

Draft a will

4.1.2 Selling

SELLING

Instruct Agent

⇩

Verify possession of all title documents in respect of property and hand copies of these to the acquirer's lawyer including utilisation licence and property plans which should be certified by the local authority

⇩

Sign Power of Attorney before a Notary or at a Portuguese Consulate

⇩

Transfer Deed *(Escritura)*

⇩

Pay capital gains at local Tax Office between March 15th and April 30th of the following year

4.2 Professional Advice

Given the substantial differences in the Portuguese legal system, full consultation with Portuguese lawyers is an essential requirement prior to signing any documentation in respect of a property.

Following the decision to buy a particular property, a preliminary legal due diligence is advisable, which would include the following being ascertained:

- Local Land Registry *(Conservatória do Registo Predial): (i)* is the vendor the rightful owner of the land, and is the land registered in his name; *(ii) is* there any mortgage, encumbrance or lien; *(ii)* are there any third party rights or interests.

- Local Tax Office *(Serviço de Finanças, da zona onde se situa o imóvel)*: *(i)* is the Annual Tax on Real Estate – IMI (*Imposto Municipal sobre Imóveis*) paid and up to date;
- Town Hall *(Câmara Municipal)*: *(i)* have the construction and/or utilisation licence been granted; *(ii)* where the plot has a construction licence, what are the future dwelling's characteristics.
- Courts or Commercial Information Companies *(Tribunais ou Empresas de Informação Comercial): (i)* is the vendor in a situation of bankruptcy, or does it have any pending criminal lawsuit that would make the alienation of its own assets ineffective; (ii) where deciding to buy a property off plan, is the constructor both capable and competent.

4.3 Search on the Land Registry

Land Registries are organised on a local basis, as aforementioned. The land registration system provides for the registration of the ownership, title, description of the property, charges, encumbrances or liens, mortgages and third party interests.

Properties must be registered at the appropriate Land Registry for the area where the land is situated.

4.4 Reservation Agreement

Reservation Agreements are becoming increasingly common when property is being sold without a previously approved construction licence.

Essentially, they are an agreement by which a vendor agrees to reserve a property for a prospective acquirer and not offer it to a third party for a given period of time, in exchange of money.

Reservation Agreements do not confer any contractual rights over the property and usually contain a clause stating that the acquirer must enter into a Promissory Contract of Purchase and Sale by a certain date. Payments made under Reservation Agreements are generally stated to be deductible from the deposits due under Promissory Contracts.

4.5. Promissory Contract of Purchase and Sale[4]

Promissory contracts of purchase and sale are widely used within conveyancing in Portugal. The promissory contract is an agreement establishing that the parties are committed to enter into a purchase contract in the future.

The main features of promissory contracts of purchase and sale of real estate property in Portugal are laid out below.

4.5.1 Requirements[5]

The key rules relating to the formalities of promissory contracts of the onerous transfer of real estate are the following:

(i) The promissory contract must be in writing;
(ii) It must be signed by both parties;
(iii) A public notary must certify the signatures of the parties and verify the existence of a valid construction and/or utilisation license.

The *ratio* behind these legal requirements is to afford the acquirer a level of protection in relation to the existence of a valid construction or habitation licence, as the case may be. The non-compliance with such requirements grants the acquirer the right to have the contract voided.

However, it is common practice that both parties agree to waive the certification of their signatures and the verification of the existence of a valid utilisation or a construction licence by a notary. In that case, the promissory contract must expressly state that both parties agree to waive all formalities, without affecting the validity of the agreement itself.

Please note that where such a clause has been entered into by the parties, in the event of any irregularities arising with the construction and/or utilisation licence, it may be argued that the acquirer shall remain bound by the terms of the contract and may not be entitled to request its voidability.

---

4 Art. 410 and 830 PCC.

5 Article 410 PCC

4.5.2 Deposit (*Sinal*)[6]

The parties may agree that, upon concluding the respective promissory contract, the promisor (acquirer) shall give the promisee (seller) a deposit (*sinal*) - usually an amount of money - which serves as a first instalment.

4.5.3 Remedies

Promissory contracts may also be subject to specific legal remedies. In the case of breach of contract by one of the parties, two mutually exclusive options will remain for the aggrieved party; the entitlement either to:

(i) Enforce the contract, in its original terms, through a court order (specific performance); in other words, the seller may require the acquirer to go through with the purchase, or vice versa, depending on which of them is in breach.

(ii) Terminate the contract and receive monetary compensation at a level in accordance with the original deposit. Note that whereas the seller would simply retain the original deposit, the acquirer may claim an amount equal to twice this sum.

In addition to either of the above, a penalty clause may also be triggered, if one has been foreseen in the contract.

4.6. Contract of Purchase and Sale of Real Estate Property (Transfer Deed)

The transfer deed is defined by the applicable provisions of the PCC as the means through which a person or a legal entity's property rights on a given asset are transferred to another, against monetary consideration.

4.7. Requirements for the Purchase of Greenfield Sites, Subdivided Properties, Properties Under Construction and Urban Properties

[6] Art 442 PCC

4.7.1. Common Requirements

The transfer must be made by means of a notarial deed which will not be signed by the public notary unless the necessary legal requirements have been satisfied.

4.7.1.1. Documentation to be Filed with the Public Notary

The following documentation must be filed with the public notary prior to execution of the deed:

(i) A registration certificate issued by the Land Registry (*Conservatória do Registo Predial*);

(ii) A Tax Office Certificate (*Caderneta Predial*) – where a stamp is provided by the Tax Office confirming the property's tax status. The stamp is valid for 12 months and may be renewed. If the property has not been registered with the Tax Office, a stamped legal duplicate of the registration application is required;

(iii) Receipt of payment of "Municipal Tax on the Transfer of Real Estate" ("*IMT*"). Assessment of this tax must be requested by the acquirer at the competent Tax Office and paid before the deed of transfer takes place. The *IMT* is levied on the taxable value of the property in accordance with the tax rates indicated below in item 6.

(iv) Utilisation Licence (*Licença de Utilização*) - A notarial deed relating to the purchase of a building or part thereof will only be executed if the public notary verifies that the utilisation licence has been granted by the municipal authorities. Please see below detailed information on utilisation licence requirements and features. (item 4.7.5.2)

4.7.1.2. Registration of Transfer Deed with the Land Registry *(Conservatória do Registo Predial)*

The transfer of property rights to the acquirer is only completed upon registration of the transfer deed with the Land Registry.

The transfer deed confers ownership of the property to the acquirer, but until such time as it has been registered it is enforceable against the seller only, and not against third parties.

In addition to a legalised copy of the transfer deed, the applicable Land Registry form must be completed and a property tax certificate produced.

4.7.1.3. Pre-Emption Rights *(Direitos de Preferência)*

At such time as a given property is offered for sale, the owners of adjacent and nearby properties or the Portuguese State may in certain circumstances have pre-emption rights which they may choose to exercise.

4.7.2. Specific Requirements for the Purchase of Greenfield Sites

There are no specific requirements with regard to the purchase of greenfield sites other than those laid out in item 4.7.1. above.

4.7.3. Specific Requirements for the Purchase of Subdivided Property

The requirements are the same as those laid out in item 4.7.1. above. However, the property subdivision licence must be presented to the public notary upon execution of the transfer deed.

4.7.4. Specific Requirements for the Purchase of Property Under Construction

The requirements are the same as those laid out in item 4.7.1. above. However, a valid construction licence, instead of an utilisation licence must be presented to the public notary upon execution of the transfer deed.

4.7.5. Specific Requirements for the Purchase of Urban Property

4.7.5.1. Form of Contract

As stated above, a notarial deed is required for the purchase of urban property. However if the purchase is for residential purposes only and transacted with recourse to a bank loan, the notarial deed can be replaced by a private document based on a Government-approved model, the parties' signatures being certified by a public notary.

4.7.5.2. Utilisation Licence (*Licença de Utilização*)[7]

As mentioned in the requirements laid out in item 4.7.1. above, a notarial deed relating to the purchase of a building or part thereof will only be executed if the public notary verifies that the said building, or part thereof, is registered with the Tax Office and that the utilisation licence has been granted by the municipal authorities, unless the property was built before 1951.

The utilisation licence certifies the conformity of the building or part thereof with the specifications contained in the construction licence and also that the property is being utilised in accordance with its proper use i.e. whether for habitation, commercial purposes, or industrial use.

For newly constructed buildings (see item 4.3 above), where permission for use has not yet been granted, the latter may be replaced by the construction licence, provided that:

(i) The transferor can prove that he has already applied for permission to use the building or part thereof;
(ii) The transferor states that:
  (a) The construction has been completed;
  (b) The construction has not been embargoed by the municipal authorities;
  (c) The construction licence has not been withdrawn;
  (d) The abovementioned application for permission (in point (i)) was made more than 50 days previously and no response from the authority has yet been received.

4.7.5.3. Property Passport *(Ficha Técnica de Habitação)*

In addition to the requirements laid out above, if the property is new and no habitation licence had been issued by August 15th 2004, a property passport,

[7] Decree Law 281/99

duly certified by the local Tax Office must be obtained. This document contains all the information concerning the property, including the names of all those involved in its construction and the building materials used. A notary will need to view the property passport prior to a transfer deed being signed.

5. MORTGAGE

Not all individuals have sufficient liquid assets to pay for the purchase of property outright. The most common method of financing such a purchase is to obtain a loan from a bank or financial institution.

Since large sums of money are involved, the lender will seek security for the money advanced and this will normally take the form of a mortgage of the property to be purchased. Therefore, through its registration, a mortgage is a security *in rem* that confers to the creditor (mortgagee) the right to be paid by the value of the property belonging to the debtor (mortgagor), having priority in relation to other creditors.

If a loan is granted to purchase a property then the mortgage to secure it will occur simultaneously with the transfer of ownership to the acquirer.

6. TAXATION AND FEES

Additional costs in buying a property include taxes on the transfer of property and fees to be paid to the Notaries and Land Registry as well as to the lawyers.

6.1. Tax

6.1.1. IMT: Municipal Tax on the Transfer of Real Estate Properties *(Imposto Municipal sobre as Transmissões Onerosas de Imóveis)*[8]

IMT is a tax that has been in force since January 1st 2004 and is payable on the transfer of real estate properties (and for that matter any right *in rem*). It is normally paid by the acquirer.

In extending the scope of taxation, the Portuguese Government is trying to prevent tax avoidance in many property transactions.

6.1.1.1. Concept of Property Transfer for IMT Purposes

A transfer of real estate property is deemed to have taken place in cases such as:

(a) If the Promissory Contract of Purchase and Sale of properties gives rise to the transfer of their possession, except where the property is the acquirer's permanent principal place of residence and the promissory contract does not comprise any of the situations targeted by the anti-avoidance measures;
(b) A lease agreement whereby the property becomes the property of the tenant upon settlement of all rental payments;
(c) Leases or sub-leases for over 30 years including those resulting from an extension of the original contract;

[8] Decree-Law 287/03 of November 12

6.1.1.2. IMT: Anti-Avoidance

For anti-avoidance purposes IMT is also payable:

(a) In cases where a Promissory Contract or an amendment thereto provides, that a buyer may assign his position to a third party.
(b) On assignment of a contract as above.
(c) On the issuance of an irrevocable Power of Attorney to sell either a property or shareholdings in a company holding a property.
(d) On the issuance of an instrument, e.g. a company resolution, coupled with a delegation of powers for the sale of a particular property.
(e) On the termination, or extension by mutual agreement of a promissory contract for the acquisition of property or exchange of property when 10 years have elapsed from the date of possession or transfer of right.
(f) On exchanges of real estate property, on the difference of the respective values.
(g) On the division of property ownership of an Estate, on the difference value between the inherited share and the remaining part of the property acquired through purchase.
(h) On the sale of water and mining rights.
(i) On the transfer of real estate property for purposes of paying up the share capital corresponding to a certain shareholding and on the allocation of real estate property to shareholders by virtue of a company's winding-up.
(j) On the acquisition of at least 75% of the share capital in a Limited Quota company holding a real estate property.

6.1.1.3. Urban Buildings / Greenfield Sites

As regards urban buildings, IMT is levied on the price of the purchase set out in the deed or on the taxable value of the real estate property whichever is the higher.

As for greenfield sites, IMT is levied on their taxable value. The criteria used for determining the respective taxable value are substantially different from those of urban buildings.

6.1.1.4. Specific Cases of IMT Assessment

IMT may be assessed differently in specific circumstances as laid out below:

(a) On the transfer of a property given as payment for a loan, either on its taxable value or, on the amount of the loan, whichever is the higher.
(b) On the 'usufruct' (the right to enjoy and benefit from the use of a property belonging to another party) if it is transferred separately from the base value of a property or vice-versa. In this case, IMT is charged at a special rate, in accordance with certain criteria laid out in a chart specifically provided for this purpose in the IMT Code.
(c) In respect of leases or subleases, on 20 times the annual rental value if equal to or greater than the patrimonial value.
(d) In respect of shareholdings or the distribution of company's assets to shareholders, on the taxable value or the value attributed to the shareholding, whichever is the higher.
(e) On the assignment of a contractual position, but the applicable tax rate will be determined according to the total consideration under the contract.

6.1.1.5. When to Pay IMT

As a general rule IMT is payable prior to the respective transaction being carried out, whether that be the signing of a deed, a promissory contract, a Power of Attorney, or assignment of the contractual position.

6.1.1.6. IMT Tax Rates

IMT is levied in accordance with the following rates:

1. Greenfield sites – 5%;
2. Urban buildings not for residential use and all other onerous transfers – 6.5%;

3. Urban buildings or parts thereof, exclusively for residential use – IMT is charged in accordance with the value of the property, as per the following practical calculation charts[9]:

(a) Owner-occupied:

Transfer value (x Euros)	Tax rates (%)	
	Tax Rate (%)	Average (€)
x ≤ 89,700.00	0	0
x > 89,700.01 and ≤ 122,700.00	2	0,5379
x > 122,700.01 and ≤ 167,300.00	5	1,7274
x > 167,300.01 and ≤ 278,800.00	7	3,8361
x > 278,800.01 and ≤ 534,700.00	8	-
x > 534,700.00	6 (single tax rate)	

(b) Tenancies:

Transfer value (x Euros)	Tax rates (%)	
	Tax Rate (%)	Average (€)
x ≤ 88,700.00	1	1.0000
x > 89,700.01 and ≤ 122,700.00	2	1.2689
x > 122,700.01 and ≤ 167,300.00	5	2,2636
x > 167,300.01 and ≤ 278,800.00	7	4,1578
x > 278,800.01 and ≤ 534,700.00	8	-
x > 534,700.00	6 (single tax rate)	

[9] Amendment made by Law 64-A/2008 of 31th December

Wherever the acquirer is resident or domiciled in a country or region considered as a "highly favourable tax system", as per a table laid out in a governmental order by the Ministry of Finance, the applicable tax rate will be 8%.

6.1.2. IMI: Annual Tax on Real Estate Property (*Imposto Municipal Sobre Imóveis*)

IMI has been in force since December 1st 2003 and is, in effect, similar to the British Council Tax. It is payable annually and during either April or April and September (two instalments) if the due tax exceeds €250, by the owner or beneficiary of the property, and is levied on its taxable value as registered at the local Tax Office.

6.1.2.1. Taxable Value

New real estate properties will have their taxable value, known in Portugal as *Valor Patrimonia*, assessed in accordance with the criteria set out by the Annual Tax on Real Estate Property Code (CIMI).

Real estate properties built and registered before December 2003 will be reassessed under CIMI following a change in ownership or, if that does not occur, after a period of 10 years.

The taxable value of urban properties, namely, residential, commercial, industrial and services-related shall be determined in accordance with following formula:

$$Vt = Vc * A * CA * Cl * Cq * Cv$$

Vt = Taxable Value

Vc = Base value of the property (Average cost of the building per square meter plus the value of the land, assessed as 25% of the building cost.)

A = Gross construction area (see below)

CA = "Use of property" weighting: residential accommodation = 1.00; accommodation = 1.00; commercial = 1.2; inside garage = 0.40; outside parking = 0.08

Cl = "Location" weighting: rural areas = 0.35; upmarket area = up to 3 but generally between 0.4 and 2.

Cq = "Quality and comfort" weighting: between 0.5 and 1.7.

Cv = "Age of property" weighting: from 0.35 (80 years) to 1 (less than 3 years).

The gross construction area is calculated as per the following formula:

A = Aa *Ab*Ac*Ad

Aa = Gross private area

Ab = Gross dependent areas

Ac = Free area up to the limit of the implantation area multiplied by two

Ad = Free area exceeding the abovementioned limit

6.1.2.3. Tax Limit Increases

Thresholds will apply to limit tax increases in the transitory period. Increases in tax payable in the following year cannot exceed:

2004 = 60 €

2005 = 75 €

2006 = 90 €

2007 = 105 €

2008 = 120 €

2009 = 135 €

2010 = 150 €

2011 = 165 €

These thresholds will not apply to properties re-assessed under CIMI, or those belonging to offshore companies.

6.1.2.4. IMI Tax Rates

The IMI tax rate is levied on the taxable value of the property as determined by the local tax authorities:

(1) Greenfield sites: 0.8%
(2) Urban buildings: between 0.4% and 0.7%
(3) New Urban buildings valued in accordance with the IMI Code: between 0.2% and 0.4%

6.1.2.5. IMI Exemption Chart

Urban buildings which are exclusively for residential use benefit from IMI exemption, as per the following chart:

Taxable value (x Euros)	Exemption period
x ≤ 157,500.00	6 years
x > 157,500.01 and ≤ 236,250.00	3 years

However, this exemption is valid only twice for the same tax payer or household.

6.1.3. Stamp Duty

6.1.3.1. Scope of Taxation

Stamp duty is levied on a wide range of deeds, contracts, documents, titles, books, papers and financial operations, covering more than a hundred deeds, contracts and operations.

Stamp duty must be paid by the person with an economic interest in the deed or contract such as the acquirer in a purchase and sale contract, credit institutions or financing companies in financial operations.

6.1.3.2. Tax rate

Stamp duty is levied on the value of each taxable deed or operation at a rate which varies depending on the type of deed or operation.

In relation to the purchase of real estate properties, Stamp Duty is levied at a 0.8% tax rate.

6.2. Fees

6.2.1. Notarial and Land Registry Fees

Notarial and Land Registry fees are always due with respect to the transfer and registration of a property.

They are determined in accordance with statutory provisions and are usually modest.

According to the latest amendments to the applicable provisions, the fees are:

(1) Transfer deed (*Escritura*): € 175
(2) Land Registration (*Registo Predial*): around € 500

6.2.2. Legal Fees

For assisting a client professionally in all necessary legal steps concerning the purchase until final completion, Portuguese lawyers normally charge a fixed fee based on the value of the property.

Legal fees which although strictly speaking should not be based on a percentage value of the property tend, at least, to be related to it.

Lightning Source UK Ltd.
Milton Keynes UK
19 April 2010

153010UK00001B/201/P

9 781904 312956